CHINA TAOIST ANCIENT QIGONG
PRENATAL ENERGY MOBILIZING QIGONG

Compiled by   *Chen Yan Feng*
                   Ke Heng
                   Xiao Xin He
Translated by *Liu Qi He*
                   Kang Shou Zhi
                   Chen Xue Shi

GUANGDONG SCIENCE AND TECHNOLOGY PRESS

First Edition 1992

Copyright 1992 by Guangdong Science and Technology Press
ISBN7- 5359- 0756- 3
Published by **Guangdong Science and Technology Press**
13F., No. 11 Shuiyin Road, Huanshidong Road, Guangzhou 510075, China
Printed by **Guangdong Xinhua Printing House**
45, Yongfu Road, Guangzhou, China
Distributed by **China International Book Trading Corporation**
21, Chegongzhuang Xilu, P. O. Box 399, Beijing 100044, China

Printed in the People's Republic of China

Publisher's Note

Chinese Qigong has a long history and a numerous and jumbled system, which can be divided into different factions and schools. But all of them originated from the three schools of Taoism, Confusianism and Buddhism. At the present time, the relatively more popular and influential ones are those of the Taoist School. The Prenatal Energy Mobilizing Qigong introduced in this book is one of the ancient Qigong exercises with unique features of Taoism.

Qigong has a systematic theory and is a self-training method of the body and mind, which was gradually understood and developed by the Chinese people in ancient times through their long-term struggle against diseases and their practice against premature aging, and through the process of productive labour and daily life. By means of practising Qigong, a practitioner can attain the aim of relaxing the body and entering a tranquillized state of mind by regulating the body

(body posture), regulating breathing and regulating the mind. Thus man's subjective initiative can be brought into full play. In a condition without the need of medication or operation and other medical treatments, Qigong practice can perform a self-regulating and self-treating function on the practitioner, and exert a supplementary therapeutic effect on many kinds of diseases.

It has been proved with modern scientific studies that Qigong is not merely a traditional therapeutic technique but also a practical means to open up the potentialities of the human body and to explore the mysteries of human life.

It is our hope that more and more people in the world can get to know about and understand Qigong, and through their own Qigong practice, attain their objectives of strengthening the body, keeping fit and preventing and treating diseases, and make Qigong a benefit to the human society.

The numbers of acupuncture points and names of meridians involved in this book can be referred to the authorized standardization in " The Location of Acupoints " published in 1990 by the Foreign Language Press, Beijing, China. Owing to the limited space, detailed explanations of the terms of Qigong and traditional Chinese medicine have not yet been provided in this book. Reference can be made to related handbooks in this field.

We hereby express our gratitude to Mr. Zeng Wei-wen of the Guangzhou College of Traditional Chinese Medicine for his careful revision of the English translation.

Spring, 1991

CONTENTS

CHAPTER I GENERAL INTRODUCTION ········ 1
CHAPTER II ESSENTIALS OF QIGONG PRACTICE ································ 11
1. Rules in Qigong Practice ································ 11
2. Notices for Practitioners ···························· 16

CHAPTER III QUIESCENT QIGONG PATTERN SERIES ························ 19
1. Body Postures for Practising Qigong ···················· 19
2. Instructions in Verse with Rhymes for Practising Qigong ·· 24
3. Prenatal Breathing (Deep Exhaling and Inhaling Pattern) ·· 26
4. Interior Revolution of Qi in Dantian ······················ 28
5. Longitudinal Revolution of Qi from Dantian ··············· 30
6. Spontaneous Revolving of the "Magic Wheel" (The Ending Pattern) ·· 33
7. Dry Washing Method ·· 34

CHAPTER IV MOTIONED QIGONG PATTERN SERIES ························ 37
JIU ZHUAN DA YUN TIAN (Nine Patterns for Inducing the Large Circulation of Qi) ·· 37
PATTERN 1 HUN DUN CU KAI(Initiating the

	Movement of Prenatal Energy) 39
PATTERN 2	YIN YANG ER QI (Inducing the Small Circulation of Qi) 44
PATTERN 3	QING TIAN YI ZHU (Promoting Ascending the Movement of Qi) 47
PATTERN 4	SHOU FEN YIN YANG (Mobilizing the Qi in the Meridians of Hand) 52
PATTERN 5	ZU LI QIAN KUN (Dredging the Meridians of Foot and Regulating the Flow of Qi) 58
PATTERN 6	JIA YAO YU DAI (Strengthening the Function of the Dai Meridian) 64
PATTERN 7	YUN ZHUAN QIAN KUN (Inducing the Large Circulation of Qi) 66
PATTERN 8	WU QI CHAO YUAN (Concentrating the Qi of the Five Zang Organs into Dantian) 75
PATTERN 9	JIU JIU GUI ZHEN (Returning Qi to Its Origin) 83
GENERAL ENDING PATTERN 85

CHAPTER V MECHANISM OF THE PRENATAL ENERGY MOBILIZING QIGONG 87

1. Meridians Involved in Pattern HUN DUN CU KAI ··· 93
2. Meridians Involved in Pattern YIN YANG ER QI 94
3. Meridians Involved in Pattern QING TIAN YI ZHU ··· 99
4. Meridians Involved in Pattern SHOU FEN YIN YANG 103

   5. Meridians Involved in Pattern ZU LI QIAN KUN ⋯ 117
   6. Meridian Involved in Pattern JIA YAO YU DAI ⋯⋯ 144
   7. Meridians Involved in Pattern YUN ZHUAN QIAN KUN ⋯⋯⋯⋯⋯⋯⋯⋯⋯⋯⋯⋯⋯⋯⋯⋯⋯⋯⋯⋯⋯⋯ 145
   8. Function of the Pattern WU QI CHAO YUAN⋯⋯⋯⋯ 146
   9. Function of the Pattern JIU JIU GUI ZHEN ⋯⋯⋯⋯ 147

APPENDICES ⋯⋯⋯⋯⋯⋯⋯⋯⋯⋯⋯⋯⋯⋯⋯⋯⋯⋯⋯⋯⋯⋯⋯⋯ 149

   1. Effects of Qigong 'Waiqi' in Electrophysiology⋯⋯⋯ 149
   2. Improvement in Visual Acuity and Increase in Vital Capacity by Practising the Prenatal Energy Mobilizing Qigong ⋯⋯⋯⋯⋯⋯⋯⋯⋯⋯⋯⋯⋯⋯⋯⋯⋯ 151
   3. Recurrence of Specific Effects of Qigong 'Waiqi' on Isolated Culture of Heart Muscle Cells ⋯⋯⋯⋯⋯ 157
   4. A Study of the Phenomenon of Film Sensitization by Qigong 'Waiqi' ⋯⋯⋯⋯⋯⋯⋯⋯⋯⋯⋯⋯⋯⋯⋯⋯⋯ 160
   5. College Students' Experiences in Practising the Prenatal Energy Mobilizing Qigong ⋯⋯⋯⋯⋯⋯⋯⋯ 166
   6. Experience of the Clinical Application of the Prenatal Energy Mobilizing Qigong ⋯⋯⋯⋯⋯⋯⋯⋯ 176
   7. Remarkable Improvement in My Cardiac Function by Practising the Prenatal Energy Mobilizing Qigong⋯⋯⋯⋯⋯⋯⋯⋯⋯⋯⋯⋯⋯⋯⋯⋯⋯⋯⋯⋯⋯⋯⋯⋯⋯ 180
   8. The Cure of My Rhinitis by Practising the Prenatal Energy Mobilizing Qigong ⋯⋯⋯⋯⋯⋯⋯⋯ 182
   9. A Letter of Thanks by a Japanese Student studying in China⋯⋯⋯⋯⋯⋯⋯⋯⋯⋯⋯⋯⋯⋯⋯⋯⋯⋯ 183
  10. Answers to the Questions from Readers ⋯⋯⋯⋯ 184

CHAPTER I
GENERAL INTRODUCTION

By Chen Yan Feng

The PRENATAL ENERGY MOBILIZING QIGONG is one of the Taoist ancient Qigong exercises in China. In the last years of the Qing Dynasty (1644–1911 A.D.), a vagrant Taoist, name unknown, from Mount Emei, Sichuan Province, came to Zhongshan County, Guangdong Province in South China to practise medicine. He soon became well-acquainted with my father Chen Xi Shen, who was then a noted physician in traditional Chinese medicine and specialized in laryngopharyngology. The Taoist taught my father the 'Prenatal Energy Mobilizing Qigong', hence the origin of this Qigong. At the age of seven, I began to study the doctrine of Taoism and learn Chinese boxing and Qigong under the guidance of my father. Through my Qigong practice in the past several decades, I deeply understood that the Prenatal Energy Mobilizing Qigong has unique and incomparable characteristics in cultivating Qi (vital energy) and in reinforcing physiologically the congenital essence and cultivating Yuan Qi (primordial energy) besides its effects of strengthening the body and treating diseases. It will not cause any deviations and abnormal reactions to Qigong during practice. As far as the location of Dantian is concerned, which is generally located half Cun below the navel and one to three Cun in depth where Qi is accumulated and cultivated in Qigong practice. There is a physiological distinction between males and females. The Dantian area in males is located above the pubis, i. e the area between the superior border of the pubis and the point Guangyuan (RN5), while that in females, below the navel, between the points Shenjue (RN8) and Guangyuan (RN5). Moreover, the practitioners of this Qigong are required only to follow the method of 'Concentrating the Tranquillized-mind and Imagining an Interior Vision', which is different from the traditional method of 'Concentrating the Mind on Dantian' because this Taoist Prenatal Energy Mobilizing Qigong involves not only the mind-concentration on Dantian but also imaginary revolution of Qi within a white light ring in the Dantian area. Thus, it can easily achieve the effect of reinforcing the accumulation of Qi and quickly acquire the Qigong sensation so that the Yuan Qi (primordial energy) can be invigorated and reinforced, which in turn favours the building-up of the body and prolongs the life span.

The Prenatal Energy Mobilizing Qigong has a whole set of methods for practice, which is divided into different series with distinct and gradual development. For instance, in the Primary Qigong Patterns, the Prenatal Breathing Method (abdominal breathing) is adopted. It not only serves as the preparation for the method 'Descending the Concentrated-mind to Dantian' but also lays a foundation for practising other 'Deep Exhaling and Inhaling' patterns. The pattern 'Interior Revolution of Qi in Dantian' serves as the basis for initial exercise of Qi, accumulation of Qi and cultivation of Qi, while the pattern 'Longitudinal Revolution of Qi from Dantian' can only be practised when practitioners reach the stage of attaining the Qigong sensation after practising the pattern 'Interior Revolution of Qi in Dantian' or when practitioners feel the initial Qi-comencement of the 'Small Circulation of Qi', circulation of Qi through the courses of Ren and Du Meridians. At this stage, practitioners should use the concentrated-mind or thoughts to induce the movement of interior Qi and activate it to circulate smoothly along the courses of the Du and Ren Meridians. The 'Nine Patterns for Inducing the Large Circulation of Qi' in

Motioned Qigong Pattern Series serves as a guide to lead Qi to get through the other six meridians after the Small Circulation of Qi is opened up. This means they are the basic patterns of the Motioned Qigong Pattern Series for opening up the Eight Extra Meridians. The practice of these patterns will stimulate the opening-up and smooth the circulation of the Twelve Meridians throughout the body. Apart from these, San Cai Gong (the pattern for integrating the essence of the heaven, human being and the earth), Xiang Yin Gong (palm-to-palm reinforcement of Qi), the pattern 'Laogong Breathing', etc. also serve as the foundation for learning to release 'Waiqi' —Qi released by Qigong master, and moreover, the pattern 'Tai Yang Gong' (sunlight absorbing for improving visual acuity) serves as a long-term supplementary practice for practitioners. The instructions in verse with rhymes for practice of the Prenatal Energy Mobilizing Qigong will lead practitioners to enter a complete self-forgetting and a visionary state of mind. Air, light and water, these last three words in the versicle reveal the supreme stage of the practice of the Prenatal Energy Mobilizing Qigong. Hereinafter, I would like to introduce, in particular, a treasure— the principle for Qigong practice—to you for preventing deviations, abnormal reactions to Qigong practice. There are only six words in this principle; being upright, relaxed, tranquillized, empty, fearless and ignoring. If a practitioner can faithfully comply with this principle, he will be ensured to keep himself away from mistakes and deviations in the course of Qigong practice and will surely succeed in achieving the supreme goal of Qigong practice.

The Prenatal Energy Mobilizing Qigong lays great emphasis on putting tranquillity in the first place and motion in the second. It is advisable not to pursue movements in shape but motion in the interior. What you have to do is just to go so far as free flow of Qi and blood in meridians is achieved. The purpose of emphasizing on tranquillity is to keep the normal physiological functions of the body and free practitioners from deviations. It is also advisable not to pursue outward movements of the body. Some people consider outward movements as the act of achieving Qigong sensation and a kind of treatment for diseases. This is not definitely right. There will be occasional movements during practice. Reaching a completely relaxed, tranquillized and visionary mental state during practice, a practitioner will have a feeling of losing his body gravity. This is a natural phenomenon which is somewhat related to the practitioner's own bodily physiological and pathological condition. For instance, if a practioner is suffering from shoulder pain, there might be a movement of the shoulder. If the lumbar region is diseased, the waist might sway spontaneously. During the course of practice, those with excess heat syndrome in the interior of the body may feel like lying on the ground absorbing the Yin Qi of the earth. Those who are in gloomy and suppressed mood would feel like uttering sounds and even crying. These are all normal phenomena that will happen in the course of practice. They are spontaneous movements closely related to the diseases of the body. Influenced by the other information coming from the outside world during Qigong practice, some people say that only outward movements of the body can indicate the achievement of Qigong sensation and the diseases are being treated. But I would not agree with them. Here I would like to make my points clear with the following questions; Can a person suffering from heart disease move violently? Can a patient with hypertension stand strenuous movements? The answers are clear. We should apply dialectic thinking in dealing with these body movements. Abnormal phenomena should be put under control promptly regardless of the influence from the outside world so as to prevent deviations. All through the history, those who believed in Taoism and sought ways to keep themselves in good health could not disregard the principle; only by being relaxed, mentally tranquillized and self-forgetting and natural can practioners get on the right way to enter the visionary state of mind. It is not strange that a variety of phenomena of Qi and movements of the body will inevitably occur during Qigong practice. I hope the six-word principle; being upright, relaxed, tranquillized, empty, fearless and ignoring for practising the Prenatal Energy Mobilizing Qigong will be of some help for you in your practice.

As these are the cases of body movement, how about the proceeding of Qi phenomena? According to the principles passed on to us by our ancestors, there are three points to follow; 'So far as mind-concentration is achieved, Qi will also be mobilized and accumulated if a visionary and nothingness state of mind is reached,' which means that the mind concentration plays a leading role in achieving the Qigong sensation. But the arrival of Qigong sensation depends upon the practitioners' entrance of visionary mental state. Practically speaking, at the beginning of Qigong practice, although practitioners are required to rid themselves of distracting thoughts, they should, however, keep thinking slightly of an imaginary interior revolution of Qi in Dantian. Secondly, it is right for a practitioner to feel as if he were in a completely relaxed and visionary and nothingness state of mind. But when the Qigong sensation emerges, and Qi gets mobilized and starts moving in the interior, the concentrated-mind should follow the circulation of Qi without slightly conscious control over it, just follow the movement of Qi to wherever it flows. Only by doing so can practitioners pass on to the stage of cultivating vitality. From this stage, practitioners will further perfect their skills in practice. With further development, then comes the visionary and nothingness state of mind. There would be an obvious distinction among these four stages; mind, Qi, Shen (vitality) and vacuity. Under no circumstances can anyone overstep these stages. The reason will be understood only after quite a long period of practice. It is forbidden for a practitioner to compel himself to practise. Compelling will not achieve anything. By contraries, it will disorder the circulation of Qi and blood in the meridians. The Prenatal Energy Mobilizing Qigong, all through the ages, was never allowed to pass on to disbelievers of Taoism according to the Commandments of Taoism, nor was there any literal record. Even if it was taught, it could only be taught by personal demonstrations as well as oral instructions. Moreover, practitioners were prohibited to demonstrate the Prenatal Energy Mobilizing Qigong in public. Those who were indulged in self-exaggeration and had minor offence would be given punishment. Those with severe offence would be driven away from the Taoist temple by the head master and be forever deprived of the opportunity to learn this Taoist Qigong, while those who were successful in the practice would have acquired sufficient interior Qi and would be ready to release 'Wai Qi' to treat diseases and save the sick. Accumulating boundless beneficence and virtue is also the motto of Taoism.

Today, the Prenatal Energy Mobilizing Qigong is introduced by me to the outside world. It has brought about great benefit to building up the health of the people, and so far not a case of deviation has ever been observed. I am introducing this Qigong Series to the public by breaking the Taoist rules in the sole purpose of spreading it to serve the betterment of people's health and bring benefit to the mankind and at the same time building up merits and virtues. My ancestors would somewhat forgive me as I expected. What I introduce and illustrate in the present form of book is the Elementary Qigong Patterns for those who are keen on the Prenatal Energy Mobilizing Qigong and those who are succeessful in their practice. If you are lucky enough, I would proceed to introduce to you the Intermediate Pattern Series of the Prenatal Energy Mobilizing Qigong. Supports to the research into this Qigong from all circles of society are expected and will be much appreciated.

CHAPTER II
ESSENTIALS OF QIGONG PRACTICE

1. Rules for Qigong Practice

The rules for Qigong practice are, in fact, the principles for the practitioners to follow and comply with and also the guidance directing practitioners to practise Qigong in a correct way. The principle of the Prenatal Energy Mobilizing Qigong has only six words, which is the significant foundation of Qigong practice. So long as practitioners bear it in mind, no deviations will occur. 'The spontaneous revolving of Magic Wheel requires no human efforts'. Just follow the rules of development, when time comes, will come success.

(1) Being upright, relaxed, tranquillized and empty.

Being upright denotes two inherent meanings. The first means having a good motive before engaging in

11

or during Qigong practice, which also means that one should first of all put in the right place the aim of his engagement in Qigong practice. Practitioners should make it clear that the purpose of practising Qigong is to strengthen the body and treat diseases but not in sole pursuit of releasing 'Waiqi' or acquiring the ability of seeing through objects. Qigong practice requires whole-hearted engegement. Practitioners must follow the principle of gradual proceeding. It is true as a Chinese saying goes, 'Constant efforts yield true success'. Therefor, do not be overanxious for quick results.

In addition, the body should be kept upright. The three points, Bainhui (DU20), Huiyin (RN1), perineum and Yongquan (KI1) should be perpendicularly connected in a straight line. Relax the muscles, avoiding stiffness of the joints, slanting of the body and bending or lifting up the head, etc.

Being relaxed means the body should be relaxed in a way like a weeping willow twig. The mind should be at ease. Be selfishless and fearless, without lust and pursuit of fame and money. Smooth out the eye bows and close the eyes with a smile on the face. The body should be completely relaxed and naturally limbering up.

Mastering the method of relaxing is of great help in grasping the main points of movements and practising Qigong well. The practice of Prenatal Energy Mobilizing Qigong calls for relaxation or limbering-up of the body. Practitioners are required to relax the whole body, the head and face, neck, shoulders, upper limbs, chest, the back, abdomen, waist, hip, knees and feet. Above all, the muscles of the whole body, the nervous system, blood vessels, joints and each internal organ should be kept in a completely relaxed state. Only when a practitioner manages to relax the body but not slacken, can the Qi and blood in his body circulate unobstructively, reaching the aim of strengthening the body and treating diseases.

The state of being completely relaxed can only be experienced by the practitioner himself in the gaseous state of Qigong after a period of practice.

Being tranquillized means that the state of mind should be as steady as an old pine standing firml on the rocky cliff. A practitioner is required to keep a peaceful and quiet mood, get rid of distractions of all sorts, concentrate all thoughts, turn a blind eye to what he sees and turn a deaf ear to what he hears so as to enable the brain to enter a tranquil, visionary and pleasantly relaxed state.

Being empty means a mental state of complete emptiness. Everything in the universe seems obscure and invisible. There is no lust and ambition. Practitioners should feel oblivious of himself, forgetting everything, and be perfectly peaceful and leisurely with broad mind as if he had come into a tranquil visionary world where all things were in the primitive state of the universe. That means during Qigong practice, practitioners should manage to feel as if he had heard nothing, not a single sound from the outside world and he were free from interference of distracting ideas and thoughts, enabling the whole body and mind to reach a visionary and empty extent.

(2) Being fearless.

Without selfish intention and personal ambition, a person can become dauntless. Being fearless means a practitioner should manage to pay no attention to noises coming out of the neibouring surroundings, and keep a firm belief in the science of Qigong and persist in regular practice. Facing various sorts of outward body movements happening in the course of practice, practitioners should not be scared but be obedient to the natrual and spontaneous movements of the body so as to meet the demand and physiological regularity of the body functioning.

Be sure not to practise Qigong intentionally and reluctantly and neither be scared by the hallucination occurring in the course of Qigong practice nor be scared by the normal phenomena; feelings of hotness, numbness, soreness, swelling, coldness and itching. These feelings will appear and disappear spontaneously.

(3) Ignoring

Ignoring means in the course of practising Qigong, facing various kinds of gaseous states, a practitioner should fear neither the outward body movements due to reactions to Qigong nor the hallucination, abnormal phenomena taking place in the practice. He should only keep practising whole-heartedly according to the correct instructions and methods, and pay no attention to what has happened. The correct attitude is that a practitioner should neither hope something would happen nor be scared by what is happening, taking a laissez-faire attitude and following the tendency of natural development. Paying particular attention to these reactions means if acting upon them with mind, the practitioner will be easily misled, deviations will occur. He will even be spellbound by hallucination.

2. Notices for Practitioners

(1) It is advisable to eat something such as dim sum, cakes, biscuits, etc. before practising Qigong. But be careful not to be overfull, or if you prefer, drink some hot water or milk but eat nothing. Qigong practice is prohibited an hour before or after meals because practising Qigong with an empty stomach will easily increase the peristalsis of the stomach and intestines, giving rise to hunger reflex, affecting mind-tranquillization. If you practise Qigong immediately after meals, owing to the fact that the stomach is still fully extended and overloaded, this is detrimental to heart-regulating and breath-regulating. This will also affect mind-tranquillization.

(2) After getting up in the morning, you should relieve yourself before starting Qigong practice, for eliminating the turbid gases will in turn help take in more fresh air.

(3) Before practising Qigong, the first thing you should do is to stabilize your mood, to stop activities of any kinds and the thinking process. Life and work should be kept in regular rhythm so as to ensure adequate and sufficient rest and sleep.

(4) It is advisable to choose a place with relatively peaceful and secluded surroundings for practising Qigong, where light should not be too strong and air should be fresh and clean and well ventilated. Be sure to prevent great noise to avoid being startled in the course of practice. In case of being scared, do not be upset and nervous. Try your best to keep calm and stabilize your mood as soon as possible. If you feel it hard to keep calm again, cease your practice and do not go on reluctantly.

(5) Practising Qigong, a practitioner should take a comfortable, upright posture. All parts of the body should be naturally relaxed. Breathing should be natural and gentle. Do not breathe intentionally and reluctantly to prolong or shorten the length of respiration.

The mind should not be over-concentrated. It should be in a state of faint concentration. Do not try intentionally to imagine different kinds of feelings and sensations.

(6) A practitioner who has not been engaged in Qigong practice for long and is not skillful enough should not be allowed to practise several Qigong exercises alternatively. Moreover, he should not have a mixed practice of different Qigong exercises to meet his

personal needs. As a proverb says, 'A rolling stone gathers no moss', he should never be in blind pursuit of variety of methods, nor in blind and unilateral pursuit of releasing 'Waiqi', or indulge himself in practising Qigong regardless of day and night and fatique. Otherwise, he will not only waste a great deal of time and energy but also never accomplish anything because of his failure in mastering the essentials of Qigong practice, or even cause unnecessary malady or Qigong deviations.

(7) Do not practise Qigong when feel restless or in a bad mood. Female practitioners are forbidden to practise during the menstrual period.

(8) Qigong practice requires perseverance. Practitioners must follow the principle of gradual development and make persistent efforts in the practice.

(9) Do not be conceited and arrogant. Do not compel yourself to practise Qigong when you do not feel like practicing it. Every practitioner should try his best to cultivate his morality and practise beneficence to accumulate merits and virtues.

CHAPTER III
QUIESCENT QIGONG PATTERN SERIES

1. Body postures for Practising Qigong

In the Primary Qigong Patterns of the Prenatal Energy Mobilizing Qigong, there are three fundamental patterns: standing, lying and sitting, the standing one being the chief.

(1) Standing Pattern

Be fully conscious and composed. Preserve a tranquillized mind with the clothes and belt loosened. First, stand with legs shoulder-wide apart, toes outward and slightly gripping the grounds, knees a bit bent, head erect, eyes slightly closed and looking forward, lips naturally closed, tongue-tip gently touching the upper palate, the inside of the point Renzhong (DU26). Wear a smile with brows smooth out and a perfectly relaxed air. Relax the shoulder with arms hanging down naturally. Contract the anus and slightly lift the perineum, the external genitalia and the anus are slightly contracting simultaneously. Ease yourself and relax the chest and abdomen. Shift the weight between the feet, a bit towards the front. Keep your body upright, relaxed, and your mind tranquillized and empty. Generally, it is advisable to face the south while practising Qigong.

(2) Lying Pattern

The main postures in this pattern are much the same as those in the Standing Pattern. Lying Pattern is subdivided into two: Supine Pose and Recumbent Pose. The requirements for the Supine Pose are detailed as follows:

Fig. 1

Lie on your back on a bed, the pillow being of moderate height, with the face upward, head naturally erect, eyes lightly closed, tongue touching the upper palate, the inside of the point Renzhong (DU26), lips gently closed, palms on the lower abdomen naturally. Slightly bend the knees and draw in the feet a little. Relax the whole body and breathe naturally (Fig. 1).

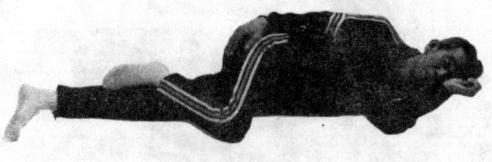

Fig. 2

Fig. 3

Recumbent Pose: Lie on your side, right or left. If the right-side pose is taken, slightly bend your left leg and place it on your right leg. Put the left hand gently on the hip with the palm downward so that the whole body becomes a little bent. Lightly close your eyes and mouth. Posturize yourself naturally and comfortably (Fig. 2、Fig. 3).

Fig. 4

(3) Sitting Pattern

Sit on a chair or a stool, naturally relaxing the whole body, holding your trunk upright not stiffly but comfortably with the neck erect. Keep the point Baihui (DU14) and the point Huiyin (RN1) in a vertical line, with the hands naturally drooping down on the two sides of the lower abdomen, feet flat on the ground, toes outward, legs shoulder-wide apart, the thighs being at a 90° angle with the shanks. The other requirements are the same as those in the Standing Pattern (Fig. 4).

2. Instructions in Verse with Rhymes for Practising Qigong

Tranquillity of mind makes me live long,
Smiling keeps me always young.
I am air,
I am light,
And I am water,
With the breeze I drift,
Far and wide.

The instructions in verse for practising the Prenatal Energy Mobilizing Qigong, though short, is very important. Reciting the verse silently before practising Qigong will help you not only to get relaxed but also to cultivate good mentality. Moreover, silent chanting can help you quickly enter a tranquillized state of mind, which is a mental environment suitable for practising Qigong. In view of the methods for Qigong practice, the silent chanting of the verse itself is a way of self-cultivating. A smiling face and a tranquillized mind readily lead the practitioners to get rid of distracting thoughts and enter a quiet and peaceful mood, and reach the lustless extent of state of mind. So the function of the verse should never be neglected.

While practising the Prenatal Energy Mobilizing Qigong, the practitioners can chant the verse in mind after posturizing. Repeat slowly each sentence in silence two to four times, imagining the scenes described in the verse. For instance, when reading 'Tranquillity of mind makes me live long, smiling keeps me always young', imagine that the whole body—muscles, nerves, meridians, joints, blood vessels, organs, etc., is relaxing naturally to the greatest extent. Close your eyes and smooth out your brows. Be calm and sedate with a smile on the face, and imagine you are as young and vigorous as ever.

While reading 'I am air', imagine yourself resolving into a breeze and merging into a single whole with the air as if you were entering a visionary mental state of nihility. While reading 'I am light', imagine again and again before your eyes there appears a white light which gradually turns into an expanse of whiteness, bit by bit you are swallowed up in. While reading 'I am water, with the breeze I drift far and wide', imagine that you are water, clear and transparent, drifting with the breeze in warm surroundings in winter or cool surroundings in summer.

In short, silent chanting of this verse makes you feel relaxed and pleasant and leads you into a peaceful, visionary, self-forgetting and tranquil world. And then move on to the practice of the Prenatal Breathing (Deep Exhaling and Inhaling Pattern).

3. Prenatal Breathing (Deep Exhaling and Inhaling Pattern)

Prenatal Breathing or a deep abdominal exhaling and inhaling is adopted in the practice of Prenatal Energy Mobilizing Qigong. The method is as follows:

Protrude the lower abdomen while inhaling and let it sink in while exhaling. Imagine that Qi is conducted into Dantian during breathing. An exhalation and inhalation is called one breath. Eight breaths are taken in the first stage of the practice. After a period of training, if no pains are felt in the abdomen and no discomfort in the chest, the number of breath can be increased step by step up to twelve, twenty-four and thirty-six. If no pains are felt in the chest and abdomen, practitioners are said to have adapted themselves to this breathing method. Each time when practising the Prenatal Breathing, the first three breaths should be taken with nose-inhaling and mouth-exhaling, the rest can all be taken with nose-inhaling and nose-exhaling. When the Prenatal Breathing Pattern is practised, it is not the strength but the mind that is used to control breathing. What we call 'inhale but not in full, exhale but not to the full' is to inhale 80% and exhale 60%. Do not exhale and inhale too deeply and too fast. Be sure not merely to pursue deep breathing. The inhaling should be fine, slow, long and profound. But you should follow the principle of gradual development. At the beginning, since the respiratory interval is short and the respiratory volume is small, the breathing appears shorter and faster. Only after a long practice can the breathing skill be perfected and naturally the breathing will become fine, slow, long and profound. Be sure to follow its natural development. Do not be overanxious for quick results. More haste, less speed. If the abdomen is forced to distend and to sink in too much in an attempt to gain sensation of Qi, it will result in distending pain in abdominal muscles and deviation will occur after a certain period of practice. On the contrary, the proceeding of Qigong practice will be affected.

The Prenatal Breathing Pattern is one of the important primary patterns in Qigong practice and also a key to success in Qigong practice. It mainly aims at helping practitioners to tranquillize their minds, store Qi in Dantian and make preparations for practising the pattern 'Interior Revolution of Qi in Dantian' and the others. Appropriate importance must be attached to it.

4. Interior Revolution of Qi in Dantian

(1) Location of Dantian

In terms of Qigong theory, Dantian is considerd as a furnace where 'elixir' is tempered. In the practice of Prenatal Energy Mobilizing Qigong, Dantian, about the size of an apple, is located between the navel and the pubis. In males, it is located between the superior border of pubis and the point Guangyuan (RN5). In females, between the point Shenjue (RN8), the navel and Guangyuan (RN5).

(2) Methods for Practising Interior Revolution of Qi

Concentrate your mind on Dantian and imagine there is a mass of Qi in Dantian, revolving within a white light ring at an even speed, a speed of clock pendulum (one turn per second). Imagine that the white light ring first revolves 36 turns clockwise and then 36 turns counterclockwise. Every 36 left turns and 36 right turns is considered as a round. After a round, make a pause for about three to sixty seconds, then begin the next round. Each time do four to eight rounds. Be sure to keep your concentrated-mind circling along with the Qi revolving in the light ring.

(3) Points to Remember

While practising this pattern, remember not to concentrate your mind strongly but faintly on Dantian. Do not think about starting the second turn with the first one unfinished. If you are absent-minded and forget the number, start once again from the beginning. In the first stage of the practice, if the circle does not follow the mind, you can make a pause for a little while, then restart from the beginning. Practitioners should rather control the circle than follow it. In addition, the number of clockwise revolving must be equal to that of counterclockwise revolving in order to keep the balance of Yin and Yang.

If the revolving ceases, stop to find out what has taken place in Dantian. When practitioners are perfecting their skills in practising the pattern of Interior Revolving of Qi, step by step, there will occur a sensantion of distention, warmth and hotness in Dantian. Eventually, Dantian will become full to the brim. The Qi in it is strong enough and overflowing, which indicates the initial fulfillment of the practice of the pattern 'Interior Revolution of Qi in Dantian' and the interior Qi has been reinforced and replenished. Practitioners can move on to the next step: to practise the pattern 'Longitudinal Revolution of Qi from Dantian'. The length of the practice varies from person to person.

(4) Functions

'The Interior Revolution of Qi in Dantian' is the fundamental pattern in the Prenatal Energy Mobilizing Qigong. At this stage, the mind is trained to concentrate on where it is needed. By way of revolving, the Qi derived from refined substance in all parts of the body is collected and accumulated into Dantian to cultivate and reinforce the Yuan Qi (primordial energy).

5. Longitudinal Revolution of Qi from Dantian

(1) Warming-up Exercises

Every time before practising this pattern, practise the pattern 'Interior Revolution of Qi in Dantian' four to eight rounds.

(2) Scope of the Longitudinal Revolving

Revolve the white light ring in the pattern 'Interior Revolution of Qi in Dantian' onto a longitudinal plane coinciding with the Ren Meridian in the front and the Du Meridian at the back, connecting the top of Dantian and the perineum below.

(3) Methods for Practising 'Longitudinal Revolving of Qi'

Concentrate your mind on the revolving white light ring in the pattern 'Interior Revolution of Qi in Dantian', revolve the Qi-mass along the ring forward, downward, backward and upward, forming a longitudinal revolving turn. A thirty-six-turn revolution is regarded as one round. After an interval of three seconds to one minute, start revolving the next round.

(4) Points to Remember

Only when sufficient Qi is accumulated after the fulfilment of the practice of 'Interior Revolution of Qi in Dantian' can the practitioners do the pattern 'Longitudinal Revolution of Qi from Dantian'. Take great care not to revolve counterclockwise, otherwise the practice will be misled and deviations will occur.

(5) Functions

The practice of this pattern aims at replenishing

Dantian with Qi and dredging the Ren and Du Meridians, thus lays a foundation for opening up the 'Small Circulation of Qi'. Gaining perfection in practice step by step, practitioners can feel Qi sensation ascending from the Du Meridian, which indicates the fulfilment of the 'Longitudinal Revolution of Qi from Dantian', that is to say, the Yuan Qi has begun its Small Circulation. This process will be long or short according to different individuals and different results achieved in the practice.

Moreover, practising this pattern plays a role in self-treatment of diseases by the sick and helps restore the health. The practical way is to take advantage of the momentum of Qi to lead it with the mind to make an attack on the focus in the diseased parts when Yuan Qi is felt replenished and vigorous after the successful fulfilment of this pattern. Generally speaking, the Qi-mass is led to revolve around the diseased parts or the diseased Zang or Fu organs. Whether a corresponding reinforcing or reducing therapeutic method is taken depends upon the nature of the illness and the type of the syndrome, deficiency or excess. Revolving to the left is reinforcing, while revolving to the right is reducing.

Every 36 turns is considered as a round. After

a round, make a pause of about three seconds before starting the next. Each time make four to eight rounds. Then cease your practice by practising the Ending Pattern.

6. Spontaneous Revolving of the 'Magic Wheel' (The Ending Pattern)

(1) Scope of Revolving

Take the abdomen and the chest as a plane with the point Shenjue (RN8), the navel as its center, and the point Tiantu (RN22) and the superior border of the pubis as its two poles.

(2) Methods of Revolving

Lead the Qi with your mind out of the point Shenjue (RN8) and revolve 36 turns running from the left to the right clockwise (for females, from the right to the left, counterclockwise), enlarging the circle bit by bit during revolving until it touches the two poles at the 36th turn. Then lead the Qi to revolve 36 turns with the circle shrinking bit by bit during revolving along the same route back to the point Shenjue (RN8).

(3) Methods for Ending the Practice

Cover the point Shenjue (RN8) with palms for

a while after the Qi is revolved back to Shenjue (RN 8) . Then open your eyes, stretch your trunk and the extremities freely. By this time the Ending Pattern is finished.

(4) Functions

In order to make the Zang and Fu organs more replenished with Yuan Qi and avoid wasting and consuming, the accumulated and reinforced Qi must be drawn back to Dantian to make it nourished and reinforced by the postnatal essence. Besides, this pattern helps to accumulate and reinforce the Yuan Qi gained in the practice so that it can be used to build up the health and enable the practitioners to strengthen their resistance against diseases.

7. Dry Washing Method

Dry washing means to massage, with the remaining Qi after practising Qigong, the head, face, ears, neck, feet, hands, etc., to replenish and nourish these parts with Yuan Qi and to relax muscles and tendons, and to activate the circulation of Qi and Blood to build up the health and nourish the skin to prevent senility. The warming-up exercises are as follows:

Take advantage of the warmth from the palms

after practising the Ending Pattern, rub the palms against each other till they feel hot. Then do the following exercises:

(1) Washing the Hands

Massage and rub the hands with each other: the palms, the dorsa of hands and the fingers for five minutes or so to regulate the blood circulation in the hands.

(2) Washing the Head

Hold your fingers of each hands together and massage the head with both hands from the temple sides to the occipital bones, then up to the vertax, to the forehead, the point Yintang (EX-HN3) and massage softly the points Taiyang (EX-HN5) and turn to massage the temple sides. Repeat the massage till the vertax feels warm. Then lightly strike the head with the finger-tips.

(3) Washing the Face

Massage the forehead transversely from side to side with the left hand, then massage the face downward-upward with both hands. Massage the upper and lower eyelids from the inner canthi to the outer canthi with the middle joints of the index fingers, and from the side of the nose wings up to the bridge of the nose, to the point Yintang (EX-HN3) and the edge of hair, down to the points of Yingxiang (LI20) with the index fingers 36 times respectively.

(4) Washing the Ears

Clip the auricles and earlobes with the thumbs and index fingers and massage the inside of the auricles. Pull the earlobes several times and flick the dorsa of the ears several times with the middle fingers.

(5) Washing the Feet

First press and massage the points Zusanli (ST36) 36 times. Then from the point Zusanli down to the heels along the outer lateral side of the legs 36 times, and the points Sanyinjiao (SP6) 36 times. Then massage the points Yongquan (KI1) with palms in turn till they become warm.

In addition, it is feasible to dry wash the head only for eight to ten minutes after you get up every morning and massage the points Zusanli (S T 36) and Sanyinjiao (SP6) 100 times each and the points of Yongquan (K I 1) 200 times.

CHAPTER IV
MOTIONED QIGONG PATTERN SERIES

JIU ZHUAN DA YUN TIAN
(NINE PATTERNS FOR INDUCING THE LARGE CIRCULATION OF QI)

In the strict sense of the word, this Motioned Qigong Pattern Series is designed for those who have succeeded in opening up the 'Small Circulation of Qi' in the body, wherein practitioners learn to conduct the flow of Qi through shapes and motions and to control it with their minds so as to stimulate and open up the other Six Extra Meridians except the Ren and Du Meridians and further stimulate and open up the Twelve Regular Meridians thus to lay a foundation for the commencement of the *'Large Circulation of Qi'. For beginners who have not yet mastered the skill for inducing the 'Small circulation of Qi', what they need to do is only to practise well the movements in shape in coordination with natural and smooth breathing and relaxation of the four limbs. This can also produce the effect of strengthening health and preventing diseases. Only when they have succeeded in inducing the 'Small Circulation of Qi', can they further learn to conduct Qi to flow by means of movements in shapes and to guide the circulation of Qi with their minds. Therefore, be sure not to overpass the stages and force yourself to practise in a rush. Otherwise you will lose more than you gain.

    Whenever you begin practising, do begin with the contemplation of the Instuctions in Verse for Practising the Prenatal Energy Mobilizing Qigong as mentioned in the Quiescent Qigong Pattern Series. Repeat each line two to four times. Each pattern is to be practised three to nine times. From Pattern One to Pattern Eight, the preparatory postures at the beginning of each pattern are the same: hold the hands in front of Dantian with palms obliquely facing each other,

---

Notes: * The Large Circulation of Qi refers to the circulation of Qi through the routes of the meridians and collaterals all over the body.

fingers pointing forward and slightly curved as if holding a ball in between, forming a ball-holding gesture. While in Pattern Nine, 'Jiu Jiu Gui Zhen', there is no definite preparatory posture, a practitioner may as well start practising this pattern according to his individual condition so long as he reaches the extent of mind concentration following the circulation of Qi to wherever it goes in his practice.

While practising this Motioned Qigong Pattern Series, practitioners should let their tongues touch the upper palate, the inside of point Renzhong (DU26) and slightly lift the anus (contracting the external genitalia and the anus simultaneously, i.e. lifting the point Huiyin (RN1)).

PATTERN 1   HUN DUN CHU KAI

(Initiating the Movement of Prenatal Energy)

Preparatory position: standing pose with ball-holding gesture.

Fig. 5   Fig. 6

Detailed Movements: stand naturally and quiescently with the feet shoulder-wide apart, the whole body relaxed, soles flat on the ground and toes pointing forward. Hold your hands in front of Dantian, palms obliquely facing each other with fingers pointing forward and slightly curved to form a ball-holding gesture (Fig. 5).

Then turn your palms slowly upward and outward to spread both arms sideways at about the same height of your waist (Fig. 6).

Fig. 7

Simultaneously, imagine that you are opening up the Ren Meridian in the front midline of the body in sequence: opening up the face—smiling, opening up the neck—lifting up the head, opening up the shoulders—expending and moving the shoulders slightly backward, opening up the chest—expending your chest, opening the abdomen—protruding your abdomen, opening up the hips—lowering your hips a little, opening up the knees—turning your knees outwards, opening up the sole—supporting the body with the outer-lateral side of the feet and slightly lifting the inner-lateral side of the soles with the point Yongquan (KI1) off the

Fig. 8

ground. After the front part of the body are completely opened, proceed to raise your arms to about the shoulder level to form an approximately straight line, inclining the whole body slightly backward (Fig. 7).

Then, gradually turn your elbow outward, bringing the palms forward-downward, and drawing them to the front of the abdomen and close to each other. Meanwhile, imagine that you are closing the point Yongquan (KI1) —resting the feet flat on the ground, closing the knees— bringing your knees together, closing the hips—contracting and raising your hips, closing the abdomen—withdrawing your abdomen, closing the chest and closing the shoulders—moving your shoulders a bit forward and turning the elbows slowly

Fig. 9

outward-upward and tucking in the chest, closing the neck—bending your neck a bit forward. Then further turn the elbows outward-upward, bringing the dorsa of the hands to press against each other, imagining that your are opening up the Du Meridian on the back from the bottom to the vertex (Fig. 8).

While opening up the points Yongquan (KI1), gradually bend forward and lower your body till it is completely squatted down, twisting the elbows as far as possible, bringing the dorsa of the hands to press ecch other. After you are completely squatted down, insert your hands into the space between the feet and try your best to extend them towards the heels so as to bring your body and head completely bent (Fig. 9).

Straighten up your body and return to the starting position (same as in Fig. 5).

Mechanism: when a practitioner is in the primary stage of the practice, the prenatal Qi (prenatal energy) has not yet begun to flow in either of the Ren and the Du Meridian. It is merely a mass of Qi turning round and round within Dantian at the monent. This pattern aims at opening up the point Tanzhong (RN17) , the Sea of Yin Meridians and the point Dazhui (DU14) , the Commander of Yang Meridians, laying a foundation for commencing the *'Small Circulation of Qi'.

Indications: illnesses of the chest; cough, asthmatic breathing, thoracic pain and hypochondria, numbness-syndrome of the chest, palpitation, pains in the shoulders, neck and the back, and lumbago, etc.

PATTERN 2 YIN YANG ER QI
(Inducing the Small Circulation of Qi)

Preparatory Position: standing position with ball-holding gesture. Hold the hands in front of Dantian, forming a ball-holding gesture and relaxing the whole body (same as in Fig. 5) .

Note: * The Small Circulation of Qi refers to the circulation of Qi through the routes of the Ren and Du Meridians.

Fig. 10

Detailed Movements: the right heel serving as the axis, turn the right foot rightward to an angle of about 45° and shift the weight onto it to form a 'left feint-step'. Slowly move your left foot a half-step forward, changing the 'left feint-step' into the 'left bowed-step, and naturally shift the weight slowly forward onto it. At the same time, turn the palms obliquely upward and stretch your hands backward-downward alongside of the hips. Incline your head forward so as to allow it to form an oblique straight line with the head, the trunk and the right lower extremity (Fig. 10).

      Fig. 11   Fig. 12

Then, lift up the head to look up, focusing the vision on the point Yintang (EX-HN3) between the eyebows (Fig. 11).

Again, lower your head, slightly lower your body as if ready to sit down. Meanwhile slowly draw your hands from behind to the front to form a ball-holding gesture (Fig. 12).

Using the heels as the axes, first turn the right foot outward and then the left foot inward. Gradually turn your body rightward to a 45° angle. Bend the knees deep enough to form a 'Mabu', horse-riding position with feet separated.

Repeat the same movements with the left foot in

the opposite direction. Then return to the standing position with ball-holding gesture (same as in Fig. 5).

Mechanism: this pattern stresses the conducting of Qi through movements in shape and the guiding of the Qi circulation with the practitioner's mind. Since the Ren and Du Meridians are the ones dominating the Yin and Yang Meridians of the whole body respectively, therefore, dredging these two meridians means to regulate the circulation of Qi in the Yin and Yang Meridians all over the body, which is the key pattern for inducing the 'Small Circulation of Qi'.

Indications: proctoptosis, hemorrhoids, hernia, menoxenia, dysuria, emission, enuresis, sterility in males, pains in female pudendum, diseases of the cervical vertebrae and pains in the back, lumbago, etc.

PATTERN 3 QING TIAN YI ZHU

(Promoting the Ascending Movement of Qi)

Preparatory Position: standing pose with ball-holding gesture.

Fig. 13

Detailed Movements: turn the palms upward and set the fingers to point to each corresponding one, the mid-fingers touching each other. Then hold them in front of Dantian (Fig. 13).

Fig. 14   Fig. 15

Curve the fingers of both hands (Fig. 14).

Then, slowly lift the hands along the Chong Meridian up to the point Tiantu (RN22) and gradually bring the dorsa of both hands to press each other (Fig. 15).

Fig. 16   Fig. 17

Continue to lift the hands alongside the route of the Ren Meridian and ascend to the point Renzhong (DU26), the philtrum (Fig. 16).

Extend two hands a bit forward, the elbow remaining half curved, and gradually separate the dorsa from each other while bringing the palms to turn upward and the ulnar lateral sides of the little fingers to touch each other (Fig. 17). Now keeping the palms upward, separate them from each other by turning them outward while allowing the interior aspects of the wrists to touch each other. Continue to turn the palms outward–backward till the radial sides of the

Fig. 18

thumbs touch each other. Slightly incline backward and look obliquely upward, palms remaining upward and knees bent. Then separate the hands from each other sideways till they are shoulder-wide apart. Then raise the palms overhead to form a posture as if you resembled in appearance a pillar propping up the sky (Fig. 18).

Incline your body slightly forward, turn your elbows inward to bring the hands to come close to each other, first touching the small thenar eminence, then the dorsa of the hands, and then press them against each other and withdraw them to the level of the point Renzhong (DU26), the philtrum with the fingers pointing at the point (same as in Fig. 16). Then descend the hands alongside the Ren Meridian to Tiantu (RN22) (same as in Fig. 15), where you separate and move them slowly along the Chong Meridian down to the Dantian. Then flatten out the palms to let the fingers of both hands point to each other with the middle fingers slightly touching each other, palms upward (same as in Fig. 13).

Mechanism: this pattern aims at dredging the Chong Meridian and regulating the circulation of Qi and blood of the Twelve Regular Meridians.

Indications: menoxenia, sterility in females, thoracic and abdominal pains, aches in the shoulder and neck, hypotension, hernia, dysuria and dryness of the throat, etc.

PATTERN 4 SHOU FEN YIN YANG

(Mobilizing the Qi in the Meridians of Hand)

Preparatory Position: standing pose with ball-holding gesture.

Fig. 19   Fig. 20

Detailed Movements: place the dorsum of the right hand onto the palm of the left one and hold them in front of Dantian (Fig. 19).

Move the left palm away from under the right dorsum, making a half forward-upward arc (Fig. 20).

Fig. 21   Fig. 22

Place the left dorsum onto the right palm (Fig. 21). Turn your body leftward and simultaneously slide the left palm round the lateral side of the waist to the back (Fig. 22).

Fig. 23   Fig. 24

Then press the part of the hand between the thumb and the index finger onto the point Mingmen (DU4) (Fig. 23).

Move the left hand away from the point, turning the palm forward, twist the body to the right, bringing the left arm more forward-upward horizontally (Fig. 24).

Fig. 25   Fig. 26

Keep turning rightward until the trunk comes to a 45° angle to the right-front direction and then turn up the left palm with fingers pointing up, palms opposite to your face. Slowly lift up the hand till the point Laogong (PC8) on the palm is at the same height with the point Yintang (EX-HN3) (Fig. 25).

Then turn your trunk leftward, bringing the left hand to move in the same direction. When it comes to a 45° angle to the left-front direction, slightly incline rightward with your right knee bent and the weight shifted onto the right leg (Fig. 26).

At the same time, bend the left elbow to draw back the palm and then lower it alongside the Ren Meridian by moving the bent elbow in an outward arc with palm facing upward. Then put the left hand onto the right one (the left dorsum on the right palm). Then stand with the knees slightly bent (same as in Fig. 21). Repeat the same movements in the opposite direction with the right hand.

Mechanism: this pattern aims at dredging the * Three Yin Meridians of Hand, namely, the Heart, Pericardium and Lung Meridians and the**Three Yang Meridians of Hand, namely, the Large Intestine, Small Intestine and Sanjiao Meridians.

Indications: thoracic pain and hypochondria, cardialgia, vexation, cough, asthmatic breathing, coronary heart disease, hypertension, pains in the wrist, pains in the upper arm, pains in the forehead, aches over the back and shoulder, swelling pain in the neck, tooth-ache and tinnitus, etc.

Notes: * The Three Yin Meridians of Hand, namely, the Lung Meridian of Hand-Taiyin, the Heart Meridian of Hand-Shaoyin, the Pericardium Meridian of Hand-Jueyin.
** The Three Yang Meridians of Hand, namely, the Large Intestine Meridian of Hand-Yangming, the Small Intestine Meridian of Hand-Taiyang and the Sanjiao Meridian of Hand-Shaoyang.

Fig. 27

PATTERN 5 ZU LI QIAN KUN

(Dredging the Meridians of Foot and Regulating the Flow of Qi)

Preparatory Position: standing pose with ball-holding gesture (same as in Fig. 5).

Detailed Movements: shift the weight onto the right foot. Bend the right knee and stretch the left foot a half-step forward to form a *'Feint-step'. Separate

---

Note: * Feint-step refers to a pose in which the body weight is supported by one foot while the other is rested on the ground feintly without exerting any force on or just touching the ground.

Fig. 28

the hands sideways and then draw them close to each other, each with the fingers pointing to the corresponding ones. Then slowly push them downward from the left thoracic and abdominal region and then along the anterior aspect of the left lower limb (Fig. 27).

As you begin to push the hands downward, you should simultaneously begin to bend your body forward-downward till the hands reach the tip of the toes (Fig. 28).

Fig. 29   Fig. 30

Separate the hands to either side of the foot and move the left hand over the dorsum of the foot, imagining it passing through the sole and the heel. Then draw both hands upward alongside the posterior aspect of the leg (Fig. 29).

Meanwhile, gradually straighten the body. When it is fully straightened up, withdraw your left foot to its original position, and then press the right palm onto Dantain and the left onto the point Mingmen (DU4) at the back (Fig. 30).

Fig. 31   Fig. 32

Then, slide the left hand round the left lateral side of the waist to the front of the abdomen and simultaneously move the right hand off Dantian. Turn the palms upward and move them a bit forward and then hold them by the side in front of Dantian (Fig. 31).

Shift the weight onto the left foot. Move the right foot a half-step rightward and then rest it onto the ground in a 'feint-step'. Then turn the trunk rightward and at the same time, separate the hands sideways. Then draw them close to each other with the palms downward and the corresponding fingers

Fig. 33   Fig. 34

pointing to each other. Descend the palms alongside the right hypochodrium and the outer-lateral side of the right lower limb (Fig. 32).

When the hands are pushed down above the dorsum of the right foot, move them in (Fig. 33), imagining them passing through the sole to the inner-lateral side of the foot. From there, draw them upward alongside the inner-lateral aspect of the right lower limb (Fig. 34).

Fig. 35

When the hands are drawn up to the end of the medial aspect of the thighs, withdraw the right foot to its original position. Then press both plams on Dantian with the thumbs and the index fingers touching each other (Fig. 35).

Maintain this position for a while, then shift the weight onto the both feet with knees slightly bent. Repeat the same movements in the other direction. The completion of the motions on both sides is considered as one round.

Mechanism: this pattern aims at dredging *the Three Yin Meridians of Foot; namely, the Spleen, Kidney and Liver Meridians and **the Three Yang Meridians of Foot; namely, the Stomach, Urinary Bladder and Gall Bladder Meridians and relieving the depressed and stagnated liver-energy and regulating the functions of the spleen and stomach.

Indications: flaccidity syndrome and numbness of the lower limbs, obesity, beriberi, sciatica, hypochondriac pain, chronic diseases of the liver, gall-bladder, spleen and stomach.

PATTERN 6   JIA YAO YU DAI

(Strengthening the Function of the Dai Meridian)

Preparatory Posistion: standing pose with ball-holding gesture.

Notes: * The Three Yin Meridians of Foot, namely, the Spleen Meridian of Foot-Taiyin, the Kidney Meridian of Foot-Shaoyin and the Liver Meridian of Foot-Jueyin.
  ** The Three Yang Meridians of Foot, namely, the Stomach Meridian of Foot-Yangming, the Urinary Bladder Meridian of Foot-Taiyang and the Gall Bladder Meridian of Foot-Shaoyang.

Fig. 36

Detailed Movements: gently and slowly push the hands a bit forward-upward, forming three circles in the body posture: one is formed by the space enclosed in the opposing parts between the thumbs and the index fingers of both hands. Another one is formed by the space enclosed in the opposing curves of the arms. The third one is apparently formed by the superficial circumference of the waist. It is not on the body surface, to be more exact, it exists about one Cun beneath the skin (Fig. 36).

The movements are detailed as follows:

While practising this pattern, keep thinking of the third circle one Cun beneath the skin round the waist.

Imagine that your mind rotates around the circle starting from the anterior upper edge of the left ilium round the back to the right side, then to the front and back to the left lateral side of the waist. This is called one round. Rotate nine rounds running, then rotate round the waist clockwise in the opposite direction: also starting from the left side to the front, then rightward-backward and return to the left. Rotate in the same way nine rounds running.

Mechanism: this pattern aims at strengthening the function of the Dai Meridian, restraining the circulation of Qi in the Three Yin and Three Yang Meridians of Foot and regulating the flow of Qi in the Ren, Du and Chong Meridians.

Indications: lumbago, abdominal distending pains, dyspepsia, numbness and flaccidity syndrome of the lower limbs, menoxenia and leukorrhea, etc.

PATTERN 7 YUN ZHUAN QIAN KUN

(Inducing the Large Circulation of Qi)

Preparartory Position: standing pose with ball-holding gesture.

Fig. 37   Fig. 38

Detailed Movements: place the dorsum of the right hand on the left palm with palms upward and hold them in front of Dantian. Move the left foot a half-step leftward by drawing a leftward arc with it. Then move the right foot a half-step rightward by drawing a rightward arc with it. Bend the knees deep enough, but with the feet firmly standing on the ground, to form a 'Mabu', a half-sitting pose (Fig. 37).

While inhaling, move the left hand away from under the right one by drawing a forward-upward arc and hold it above the right palm; exhale while placing the left hand onto the right one, the dorsum of the left hand on the right palm (Fig. 38).

Fig. 39   Fig. 40

Natural breathing is used in all the following movements. The moving palm should always be kept upward. If there is any difficulty in doing so, you may twist or bend the lower limbs for the ensurance of success and to keep the body balance.

Turn your trunk leftward, slide the left hand round the left lateral side of the waist to the right lateral side of the waist on the back with palm upward, gradually bending the body forward (Fig. 39).

Maintain the bending position, looking at the left palm, turn the trunk rightward, bringing the left hand from behind the back to the left side (Fig. 40).

Fig. 41　　　　Fig. 42

Then move the hand forward and rightward with the palm upward. Continue to turn the trunk rightward, bringing the left hand forward, then rightward. Inclining backward, move the hand over the face with the dorsum passing over the face and palm upward. By this time, your posture should gradually change into a 'Mabu', a half-sitting pose (Fig. 41).

When the left hand moves to the left lateral side, stretch it leftward to the same height with the shoulder. Then bend the left leg and straighten the right one to form a 'left-bowed step', shifting the weight onto the left foot (Fig. 42). Slowly sweep

      Fig. 43   Fig. 44

the left hand forward. Simultaneously, bend the right leg to form a 'Mabu', a half-sitting pose, with the weight shifted to the middle (Fig. 43).

    Continue to turn the trunk rightward, bringing the left hand to the right while gradually shifting the weight to the right foot by straightening the left leg to form a 'right-bowed step' (Fig. 44).

Fig. 45   Fig. 46

Continue to move the left hand towards the right shoulder until its ulnar lateral side against the shoulder. Turn your head rightward to look at the palm (Fig. 45).

Change the 'right-bowed step' position into a 'Mabu', a half-sitting pose, and twist your waist right-backward as far as possible so as to let the waist move to a great extent (Fig. 46).

After that, turn the trunk leftward, moving the left hand off the right shoulder, and let it sweep right-forward. At the same time, gradually shift the weight onto the right foot by straightening the left leg to form a 'right-bowed step' (same as in Fig. 44).

Fig. 47

Continue to turn the trunk leftward and gradually shift the weight to the middle so that when the left hand is brought in front of the body, a 'Mabu' position is formed (same as in Fig. 43).

Continue to turn leftward and gradually staighten the right leg and shift the weight onto the left one to form a 'left-bowed step' (same as in Fig. 42). All through the procceding of movements, the left hand is always kept at the same level with the shoulders.

Then incline the trunk rightward with the face upward, and shift the weight onto the right foot. At the same time, bend the left elbow to bring the hand towards your face (Fig. 47).

Fig. 48   Fig. 49

Move the hand over the face, then stretch it out obliquely right-forward, keep the palm upward by twisting the elbow and the wrist (Fig. 48).

Sweep the left hand leftward with the body bent forward-downward and palm upward (Fig. 49).

Fig. 50

Continue to turn the trunk-leftward and move the left hand round the lateral side of the waist to the right side of the back, still keeping the palm upward (Fig. 50).

Withdraw the hand leftward, let the palm and fingers pass the point Mingmen (DU4), then round the left lateral side of the waist and back to the front of the body. Then rest the dorsum of the left hand onto the right palm (same as in Fig. 37).

Repeat the same movements in the opposite direction with the right hand to complete a cycle of the motion and keep the balance in body movement. When you finish the cycle of movements, withdraw the feet and return to the standing pose with ball-holding gesture (same as in Fig. 5).

Mechanism: this pattern aims at dredging the Three Yin and Three Yang Meridians of Hand and Foot and limbering up the joints all over the body. This is a comprehensive pattern in the Motioned Qigong Pattern Series, Jiu Zhuan Da Yun Tian, in which the Large Circulation of Qi is stimulated and induced after practitioners' success in inducing the Small Circulation of Qi.

Indications: arthralgia all over the body; lumbago, hyperplasia of the lumbar vertebrae, osteoarthritis of the cervical spine, arthralgia of the knees, periarthritis of the shoulder, distending pains in the abdomen and constipation.

PATTERN 8　　WU QI CHAO YUAN

(Concentrating the Qi of the Five Zang Organs into Dantian)

Preparatory Position: standing pose with ball-holding gesture.

Fig. 51

Detailed Movements: separate the hands sideways with palms downward. Then slowly lift them upward till they are at the same height and in an approximately straight line with the shoulders (Fig. 51) .

Fig. 52

Turn the palms upward. Imagine the points Laogong (PC8) on either palm absorbing the Qi of Heavenly-Yang and the Qi of Earthly-Yin (the cosmic Qi), which is immediately and directly transported to Dantian (Fig. 52).

Fig. 53   Fig. 54

Inhale, spinning the arms inward to the front, bringing them close to each other and inhaling the Heavenly and Earthly Qi. Simultaneously, with palms downward and fingers of both hands pointing to their corresponding ones. Hold the hands up to the superciliary ridge with the lateral side of the index fingers lying in front of the point 'Lingqiao' i.e. Yingtang (EX-HN3) (Fig. 53).

Then exhale, imagining the Qi being breathed out to Dantian. Then regulate your breath by employing the natural breathing. Inhale once again, imagining you are drawing in the Qi of the Heavenly-Yang

    Fig. 55   Fig. 56

through the point Baihui (DU20), and at the same time descend the hands alongside the route of the Ren Meridian at the same speed as the flowing of Qi. The hands alongside are descended to the front of Dantian just as the Qi is drawn into Dantian (Fig. 54).

Exhale, imagining the Qi is breathed out all the way to the point Yongquan (KI1) along either leg. Meanwhile slowly incline forward and bend over till your body is completely squatted down, bringing the hands down to press the dorsa of the feet (Fig. 55).

Turn the palms upward. Inhale, slowly straightening up with the hands moving up and palms upward (Fig. 56).

Fig. 57

Simultaneously, imagine the points Yongquan (KI1) on each sole absorbing the Qi of Earthly-Yin and the Qi being transported directly to Dantian along the legs. When your body is completely straightened up, press the palms obliquely on Dantian (Fig. 57).

Concentrate your mind on Dantian for a while with natural breathing. Then proceed to practise the Pattern 'Spontaneous Revolving of the Magic Wheel'.

Spontaneous Revolving of the 'Magic wheel'

Preparatory Position: standing pose with ball-holding gesture.

Fig. 58

Detailed Movements: lower the left hand on the left side while clench a loose fist with the right hand and press it onto Dantian. Imagine there exists a circle centering around the navel, and the top of the circle reaching the point Tiantu (RN22) and connecting the junction of the pubis at the bottom. Starting the revolving from the navel, first revolve spinally clockwise 36 turns, enlarging the circle bit by bit during the revolving until it touches the point Tiantu (RN22) and the superior border of the pubis at the 36th turn. Then revolve counterclockwise 36 turns with the circle shrinking bit by bit and the last one returns to the navel, its starting point (Fig. 58).

Mechanism: through the practice of this pattern, practitioners cultivate and reinforce the Qi, vital energy of the human body by collecting and absorbing from the universe the essence of the Heavenly-Yang and the Earthly-Yin, integrating the essence of the heaven, earth and the human being into one. Then the integrated essence is transported to the five Zang organs to reinforce Qi and blood, strengthening the function of the five Zang organs. If you persevere in Qigong practice and in time the Qi of the five Zang organs will be intergrated into one, becoming elixir of life in Dantian, from there it ascends and merges into *Ni Wan Gong, or the 'Clay-Pill Palace' in the brain. As a result, LingGuang, 'lights of inspiration', will appear in the practitioner's brain, which is a kind of special function gained through Qigong practice and the appearance of Lingguang indicates the fulfilment of the supreme stage of Qigong practice.

Functions: harmonizing the functions of the five Zang organs and treating illnesses of the five Zang organs.

Note: * Ni Wan Gong or 'Clay-pill Palace', i.e. area where the pineal body lies in the brain in modern medicine.

Appendant Table 1

Classification of the Five Elements and the State of Viscera in the Pattern Wu Qi Chao Yuan

Five Elements	Wood	Fire	Earth	Metal	Water
Five Zang Organs	liver	heart	spleen	lung	kidney
Five Sense Organs	eye	tongue	limbs	nose	ear
Five Senses	sight	taste	touch	smell	hearing
Five States	spirit	mind	mood	soul	refined energy
Five Colours	green	red	yellow	white	black

PATTERN 9   JIU JIU GUI ZHEN

(Returning Qi to Its Origin)

Preparatory Position: flat sitting pose.

Fig. 59

Detailed Movemenets: sit on the floor or a bed, the soles and toes of both feet pressing against each other with the head erect, neck relaxed, and the spinal column straightened. The palms are put together with fingers pressing against each other. For male practitioners, the right thumb overlaps while the left one stays erect, and vice versa for the female. The thumbs are held 3-5 cun away in front of the thorax with the tips of the middle fingers pointing to the chin and elbows pointing towards the knees at a distance of about 5 cun (Fig. 59). If a practitioner has succeeded in inducing and opening up the 'Small Circulation of Qi', when he practises this pattern, he can just set free his mind and let it travel along the flowing of Qi in the state of nothingness. While those who have not yet succeeded should keep on practising the pattern 'Interior Revolution of Qi in Dantian'. During the course of practice, they should try to act upon the principle for practising Qigong: being upright, relaxed, tranquillized, empty, fearless and ignoring.

Mechanism: this pattern aims at cultivating the practitioners' 'True Qi' and heightening their intelligence.

GENERAL ENDING PATTERN

After practising the Motioned Qigong Pattern Series, the practitioners are advised not to move about immediately. They are required to practise the Ending Pattern to make the Yuan Qi (primordial energy), which has already been mobilized and tempered in practice, accumulated, condensed and reinforced and the Zang and Fu organs reflenished with it so that their functions will be further strengthened. In a word, the practice of the General Ending Pattern will help heighten the body resistance against diseases. Some movements of the Dry-washing Ending Pattern are the same with those in the Quiescent Qigong Pattern

Series. The sequence of the proceeding is as follows: rub the hands till they feel warm, then dry wash the head with the fingers rubbing the head through the hair, dry wash the face: massage the face with both hands, dry wash the ears, and dry wash the neck.

CHAPTER V
MECHANISM OF THE PRENATAL ENERGY MOBILIZING QIGONG

Before a man is given a life, he is first given a form of an entity which later develops into a fetus. The fetus receives the prenatal endowment from its parents and grows in the uterus of its mother. It assimilates from its mother the acquired essence through the umbilical cord by which the Qi and blood circulate endlessly in the Ren and Du Meridians of the fetus, the Small Circulation being open at this stage.

When the baby is born, the umbilical cord is cut and Ren and Du Meridians in the baby's body are then separated from each other; the Ren Meridian is in the front, running along the front midline of the body, while the Du Meridian is at the back, running along beneath the surface of the spinal column, only leaving the Prenatal Qi, vital energy acquired from parents before birth, within the navel, which is what we call, in terms of Qigong theory, the prenatal True Qi possessed by a baby in its earliest stage of life.

The Prenatal Energy Mobilizing Qigong stresses the concentration of mind on Dantian. It aims at mobilizing the prenatal Yuan Qi existing in the navel in order to coordinate the circulation of Qi and the air inhaled in postnatal breathing to keep the balance of the Yin and Yang and coordinate the interacting functions of Fire and Water according to the Theory of Five Elements, and to link up the circulation of the Ren and Du Meridians so as to cultivate and reinforce the True Qi. It also aims at maintaining the free flow of Qi in the meridians, restoring the innateness, strengthening the body, and preventing and treating diseases, finally prolonging life. With persevering practice, some practi-tioners, though very few, might succeed in reaching the supreme extent of Qigong practice and attaining an extraordinary function. The ancient traditional Chinese medicine had long since established the conception of interacting between the heaven and human being, in which the heaven is referred as the 'large universe', while the internal environment of the human body is referred as the 'small universe'. What does universe mean after all? A Chinese scholar, Wang Xi Yu wrote in his essay

'On the Arrangement of Elements in the Universe and the Chart of Meridians and Collaterals by Zhou Yi' that, "The universe is the one composed of materials (elements). Material is the substance composing the universe. The universe is an electromagnetic field and it is the figure as well, so is the material (element). Therefore, the universe and material (element), the field and the figure are unified……". "There are in all 162 kinds of elements existing in the universe, of which 81 kinds are stable elements and the rest are decay elements. The periodic limit of the whole periodic table is 9……. The electrons of all the elements are arranged in coordination with specific programme of the standardized field." "when elements are sufficient in number for the consumption of the human body's activities, a man stays alive; if the number of elements increases, he grows; if the number of elements decreases, he gets feeble and debilitated; and with the exhaustion of elements and a sharp decrease in number, death will result. The size of the universe depends upon that of the electromagnetic field while the universe's flourishing and declining depend upon the total amount of existing elements. The life, growth, disease and death of human being are also dependent on the number of elements." Practising the

Prenatal Energy Mobilizing Qigong can cultivate and replenish the True Qi. That means to enrich the postnatal Qi and augment the prenatal Qi and to gain adequate amount of elements for the consumption of the body and to increase the number of elements for the growth of the body. In other words, it means to slow down the decreasing in number of the elements and to delay the arrival of its exhaustion.

Each pattern of the Motioned Qigong Pattern Series can be practised 9 times. There are nine patterns in all in this series and a practitioner has to practise 81 times all together for these nine patterns, which is the ideal amount for practising this Qigong. It is according to this meaning that the nineth pattern of the Motioned Qigong 'Jiu Jiu Gui Zhen' is entitled. 'Jui Jui' in Chinese means nine nine. Hence the name of the last pattern, which means nine nine returning the Qi to its origin, Dantian. (the classics 'Yi Jing' holds that 9 is the largest number of things and when the count of things comes to 9, it will restart from the very beginning).

Professor Qian Xue-shen, a noted Chinese physicist, expounds in his essay 'The Science of the Human Body: A Major Branch Among the System of Modern Science and Technology' that the science of the human body is simply marvelous, for it deals with the human body itself. The kernel of the thought in it is, in light of modern science of systematology, that the human body is a huge system. Its complexity is far beyond the large system. In the science of systematology, especially in the systematology dealing with the basic science, there are small systems, large systems and huge system in terms of system. While the system of the human body is a huge one. There exist in it many levels, the highest of them is the human body itself, existing and functioning as an entity. Such a huge system is constantly interacting and functioning with the environment around it. In another sense of the word, it is not a closed system but an open one, existing in the universe and communicating with the others. The universe is a super huge system, in which exists the huge system of the human body, an open and extremely intricated one. It is the logic of the theory that 'the heaven and human being are integrated as one'. In the broad sense, the circulation of Qi between the heaven and the earth is regarded as 'Da Zhou Tian', the Large Circulation of Qi in the universe, while the circulation of Qi within the human body in called 'Xiao Zhou Tian', the Small Circulation of Qi. The Qi, vital energy of the human body is changing along with the changes in the heaven and earth. Therefore, the changes taking place in the Qi within the human body are also interacting on the Heavenly Qi and harmonizing the Earthly Qi.

Those of mortal had to obey the natural law of the universe while those who have become supernatural being can disobey it. Perseverance in practising Qigong and successful fulfilment in reaching the supreme extent of Qigong practice will help the practitioner make the acquired essence change into the prenatal Qi. In the end, the acquired essence and the prenatal Qi will merge into a single whole. Let us study and acquire a true knowledge of the human life through Qigong practice and try to explore the mysteries of life, understand the science of human body and strengthen the functioning of life so as to control and prolong life. Hereinafter, the meridians involved in the Motioned Qigong Pattern Series, and Nine Patterns for Inducing the Large Circulation of Qi are described.

1. MERIDIANS INVOLVED IN PATTERN HUN DUN CU KAI

(1) Point Tanzhong (RN17)
(2) Point Dazhui (DU14)

The practice of this pattern mainly aims at opening up the point Tanzhong (RN17) and the point Dazhui (DU14). The point Tanzhong belongs to the front Mu Points, one of the Eight Influential Points of Qi and is one of the main points of the Ren Meridian. It is also called 'the Sea of Yin Meridians' in Chinese Acupuncture and is often referred as 'the Middle Dantian' in books dealing with Qigong. The point Dazhui (DU14) is referred as 'the caolescence point of the three yang meridians and the Du Meridian' in the "A-B Classics of Acupuncture and Moxibustion". In other books, it is also called 'the Commander of Yang Meridians'.

The word 'Cu Kai' in Chinese means to open first these two points and motivate the Yuan Yin (primordial Yin) and Yuan Yang (primordial Yang) so as to lay a good foundation for opening up the Ren and Du Meridians.

In fact, in the practice of this Motioned Qigong

pattern, the Ren and Du Meridians are also preliminarily opened, only the Qi has not yet begun to circulate through the routes of these meridians and it will start the 'Small Circulation of Qi' before the pattern Yin Yang Er Qi is practised.

2. MERIDIANS INVOLVED IN PATTERN YIN YANG ER QI

This pattern emphasizes opening up the Ren and Du Meridians.

(1) The Ren Meridian

The Ren Meridian starts from the point Huiyin (RN1), the perineum below the point Zhongji (RN3). It goes anteriorly to the pubic region and ascends along the interior of the abdomen, passing through the point Guangyuan (RN4) and other points along the front midline to the throat. Ascending further, it curves around the lips, passes through the cheek and enters the infraorbital region, at the point Chengqi (ST1).

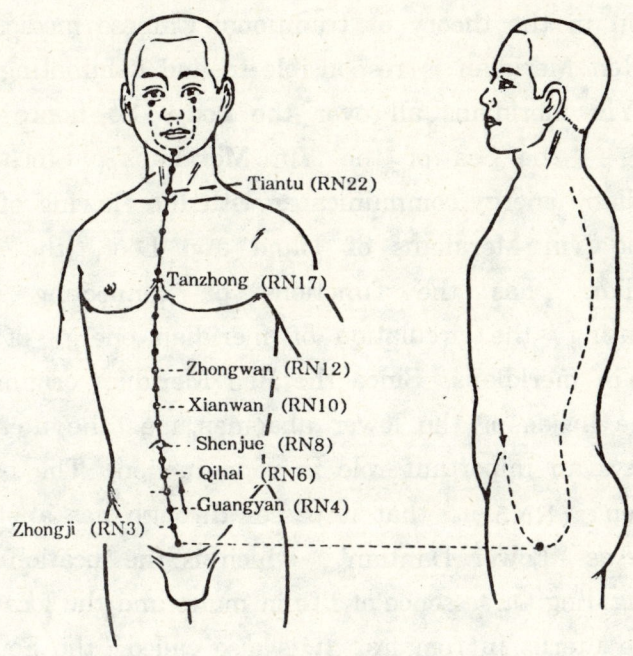

Fig. 60
The circulatory route of the Ren Meridian

The main points involved in the Ren Meridian are: Huiyin (RN1), Zhongji (RN3), Guangyuan (RN14), Qihai (RN6), Shenque (RN8), Xiawuan (RN10), Tanzhong (RN17), Tiantu (RN22) and Chenjiang (RN24) (Fig. 60).

Functions of the Ren Meridian: the word 'Ren' in Chinese means responsibility and breeding. Running along the front midline of the abdomen, which pertains to Yin in the theory of traditional Chinese medicine, the Ren Meridian is responsible to and dominating all the Yin meridians all over the body. So hence the saying 'the Sea of the Yin Meridians'. Since its meridian energy communicates with the flowing of Qi in the Yin Meridians of Hand and Foot, the Ren Meridian has the functions of connecting and regulating the circulation of meridian energy of all the Yin meridians. Since the Ren Meridian originates in the inside of the lower abdomen i.e. the uterus, it plays an important role in reproduction. The point Shimen (RN5) that it passes through has another name as 'Lower Dantian', which is the location for storing Jing Qi, essence of life in males and the location of the uterus in females. It is also called 'the Source of Production of Qi'.

In this pattern, the movements 'nodding the head and lifting the hands' mean to promote the Qi to flow along the route of the Ren Meridian and to open up it. While the movements 'lifting the head and lowering the hands' are the method to promote the Qi, through the route of the Du Meridian, to ascend from Changqiang (RN1) to pass through Dazhui (DU 14) and reach Baihui (DU20), connecting the Du Meridian.

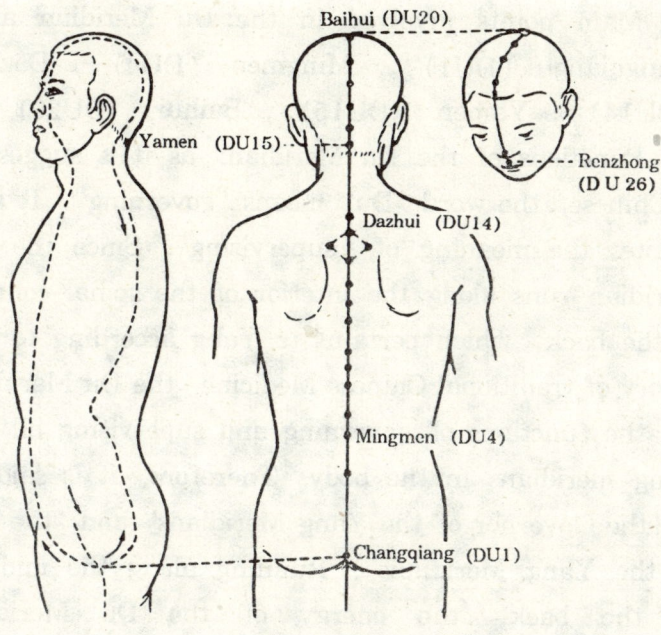

Fig. 61
The circulatory route of the Du Meridian

(2) The Du Meridian

The Du Meridian arises from the lower abdomen in the middle of the pelvis and emerges from the perineum. Then it turns posteriorly along the interior of the spinal colum to the neck, where it enters the brain. It further ascends to the vertex along the midline of the head and winds along the forehead to the columnella of the nose, passing the upper lip, and reaches the region of labial frenum (Fig. 61).

Main points involved in the Du Meridian are: Changqiang (DU1), Mingmen (DU4), Dazhui (DU14), Yamen (DU15), Baihui (DU20).

Functions of the Du Meridian: as it is suggested in Chinese, the word 'Du' means 'governing'. It also denotes the meaning of 'supervising'. Since the Du Meridian runs along the interior of the spinal column at the back, which pertains to Yang according to the theory of traditional Chinese Medicine, the Du Meridian has the functions of governing and supervising all the Yang meridians in the body. Therefore, it is said to be 'the Governor of the Yang Meridians' and 'the Sea of the Yang Meridians'. Running along the midline of the back, the energy of the Du Meridian communicates with that of the three Yang Meridians of Hand and Foot. Dazhui (DU14) is their confluence point. Besides, the Dai Meridian emerges from the second lumbar vertebra and the Yangwei Meridian communicates with the Du Meridian at the point Fengfu (DU16) and Yamen (DU15), so the energy of the Du Meridian communicates with that of all the Yang Meridians. Furthermore, because the Du Meridian runs along the interior of the spinal column and enters the brain, it is closely related to the brain and spinal cord. The medical classics "Compendium of

Materia Medica" holds, "the brain is the house of spirit and consciousness". That shows the circulation of meridian energy has a close relationship with the brain. While the Zang and Fu organs are controlled by the energy of the Du Meridian by means of the acupoints of the Urinary Bladder Meridian of Foot-Taiyang on the back. The functional activities of the Zang and Fu organs are related to the Du Meridian.

For the above reasons, the Du Meridian is also known as 'the Headquarter of the Yang Meridians'.

3. MERIDIANS INVOLVED IN PATTERN QING TIAN YI ZHU

In this Motioned Qigong pattern, the energy of the Chong Meridian begins to ascend when a practitioner curves his fingers upward and moves the hands upward alongside the Chong Meridian with fingers pointing upward.

The Chong Meridian: an ascending branch emerges at the superior part of the throat and the posterula, transporting the refined energy to the Yang meridians.

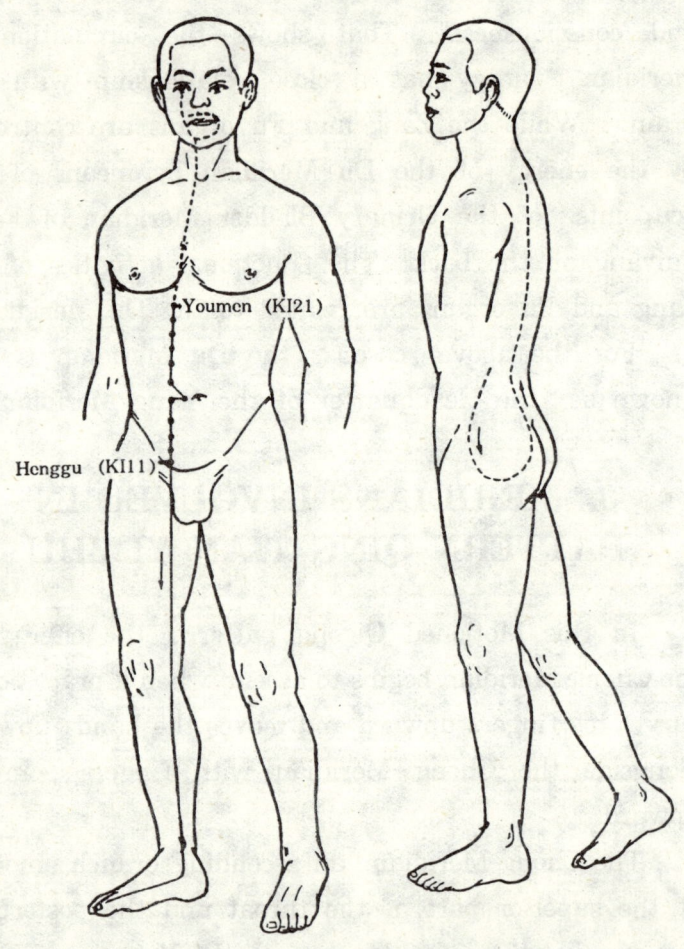

Fig. 62
The circulatory route of the Chong Meridian

Its descending branch emerges at Qichong (ST 30) region, communicating with the main collateral of the Kidney Meridian of Foot-Shaoyin. Further descending along the interior aspect of the thigh, it enters the popliteal fossa and continues to go downward along the interior aspect of the tibia deep in the shank. Reaching the superior boder of the calcaneus behind the medial malleolus of the foot, it splits into two branches: one running parallel to the Kidney Meridian of Foot-Shaoyin, transporting refined energy to the three Yin Meridians of Foot; the other branch running along the anterior aspect of the shank emerges from the superior boder of the calcaneus deep behind the medial malleolus, passing through the dorsum of the foot and entering the big toe (Fig. 62).

Among the Eight Extra Meridians, including the Du, Ren, Chong, Dai, Yinqiao, Yangqiao, Yinwei and Yangwei Meridians, only the Ren and Du Meridians have their own points distributing on their circulatory routes. The other six Extra Meridians do not have their own except the coalescent points. The Chong Meridian communicates with the Kidney Meridian at some of the points.

Functions of the Chong Meridian: The word 'Chong' bears the Chinese meaning 'vital or communications center' and 'vital communications line'. Ascending to the head and running down to the foot and communicating with all the meridians of the body, the Chong Meridian functions as the communications centre of Qi and blood of all the meridians. It can regulate the circulation of Qi and blood of the Twelve Meridians. So it is given the name ' the Sea of the Twelve Regular Meridians', 'the Sea of the Five Zang Organs and Six Fu Organs' and the name 'the Sea of Blood'. As the Chong Meridian runs parallel to the Ren Meridian and communicates with the Du Meridian, its meridian energy is transported up to and fills the Yang Meridians in the head and is infiltrated into the three Yin Meridians in the lower limbs. It, therefore, can hold the Qi and blood of the Five Zang and Six Fu Organs from the Twelve Regular Meridians. Besides, the Chong Meridian communicates with the Stomach Meridian of Foot-Yangming at the point Qichong (ST30), and runs parallel to the Kidney Meridian of Foot-Shaoyin.

The stomach is referred as 'the Source of Postnatal Energy' and 'the Reservoir of Food Stuff' and the Kidney as 'the Origin of the Innate Energy' and 'the Initial Point of the Primordial Energy'. Originating from the uterus, the Chong Meridian is called "the

Blood Chamber' and 'the Sea of Blood'. There fore, it has a close relationship with menstruation in women. The medical classics" Plain Questions" says 'When the Taichong (the Chong Meridian) is vigorous in its functioning, the menstruation comes regularly and periodically' and ' When the Taichong Meridian becomes exhausted, mentruation becomes little and even amenorrhea occurs as a result.'

This shows that the functions of the Chong Meridian are closely related to the menses and pregnancy in women.

4. MERIDIANS INVOLVED IN PATTERN SHOU FEN YIN YANG

This pattern is characterized by the movements of the hands in front of and behind the body, on the left and the right of the body. As a result, the meridian energy distributed in the three Yang and three Yin Meridians of Hand gets mobilized.

(1) The Large Intestine Meridian of Hand-Yangming

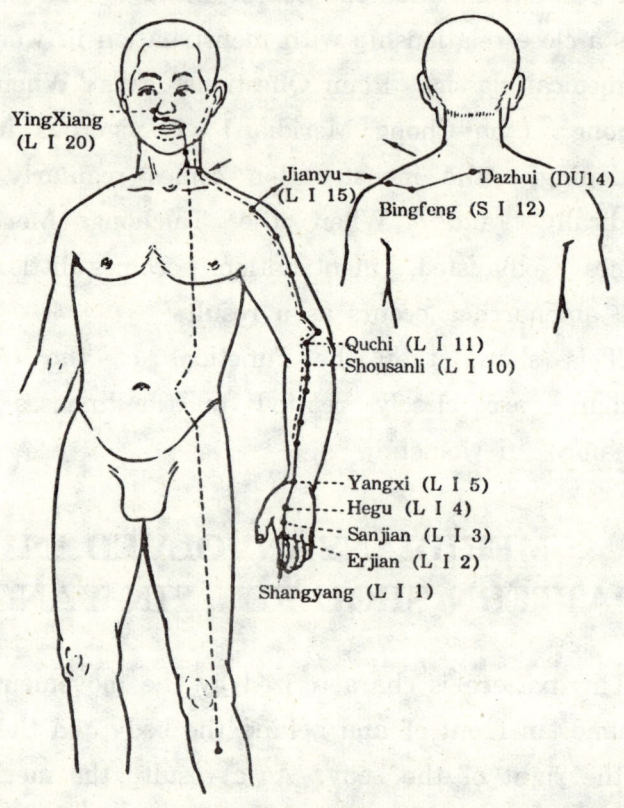

Fig. 63
The circulatory route of the Large Intestine Meridian of Hand-Yangming

The Large Intestine Meridian of Hand-Yangming starts from the tip of the index finger (Shangyang, (LI1). Running upward along the radial side of the index finger and passing through the interspace of the 1st and 2nd metacarpal bones (Hegu, L I 4), it dips into the depression between the tendons of m. extensor pollicis longus and brevis. Then, following the lateral anterior aspect of the forearm (Pianli L I 6) and (Shousanli L I 10), it reaches the lateral side of the elbow (Quchi L I 11). From there, it ascends along the lateral anterior aspect of the upper arm (Shouwuli, L I 13) to the highest point of the shoulder (Jianyu, L I 15). Then along the anterior border of the acromion, it goes up to the 7th cervical vertebra to communicate with Dazhui (DU14), the confluence of the three Yang Meridians of Hand and Foot, and it descends to supraclavicular fossa (Quepen, ST 12) to connect with the lung. It then passes through the diaphragm and enters the large intestine, its pertaining organ (Fig. 63).

The main points involved in the Large Intestine Meridian of Hand-Yangming are: Shangyang (L I 1), Hegu (L I 4), Yangxi (L I 5), Shousanli (L I 10), Quchi (L I 11), Jianyu (L I 15) and Yingxiang (L I 20).

Functions of the Large Intestine Meridian of Hand-Yangming: mainly linking up the large intestine, its pertaining organ, and the upper limbs and circulating

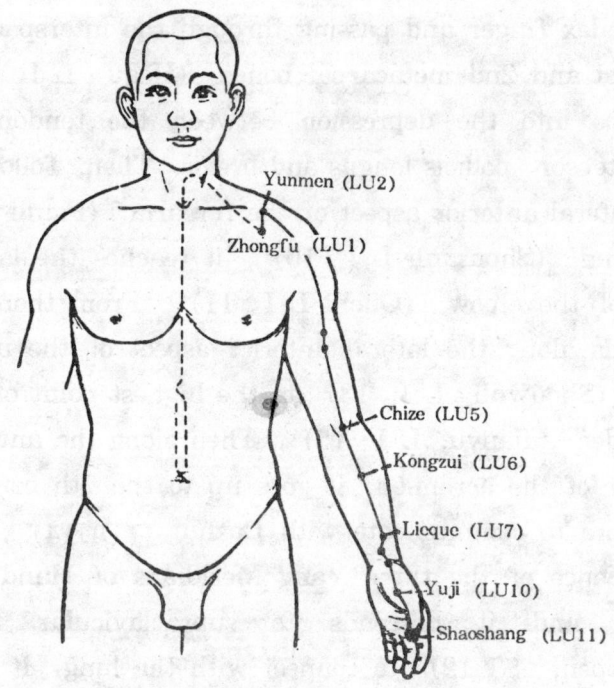

Fig. 64
The circulatory route of the Lung Meridian of Hand-Taiyin

Qi and blood to nourish all parts of the body.

(2) The Lung Meridian of Hand-Taiyin

The Lung Meridian of Hand-Taiyin originates from the Middle Jiao, running downward to connect with the large intestine. Winding back, it goes along the upper orifice of the stomach, passes through the diaphragm and enters the lung, its pertaining organ.

From the lung system, which refers to the portion of the lung communicating with the throat, it comes out transversely (Zhongfu, LU1) and goes up to the point Yunmen (LU2). Descending along the medial aspect of the forearm, it reaches the cubital fossa (Chize, (LU5). Then it goes continuously downward along the anterior border of the radial side of the medial aspect of the forearm (Kongzui, LU6) and enters Cunkou (the radial artery at the wrist for pulse palpitation). Passing the thenar eminence (Yuji, (LU10), it goes along its radial border, ending at the medial side of the tip of the thumb (Shaoshang, L. 11) (Fig. 64).

The main points involved in the Lung Meridian of Hand-Taiyin are: Zhongfu (LU1), Yunmen (LU2), Chize (LU5), Lieque (LU7), Yuji (LU10) and Shaoshang (LU11).

Functions of the Lung Meridian of Hand-Taiyin: mainly connecting the lung, its pertaining organ and the upper limbs and circulating Qi and Blood to nourish all parts of the body.

(3) The Sanjiao Meridian of Hand-Shaoyang

The Sanjiao Meridian of Hand-Shaoyang originates from the tip of the ring finger (Guangchong, S J 1), running upward along its lateral side and reaches the dorsum of the hand. Emerging from the dorsal aspect of the wrist, it runs upward along the lateral aspect of the forearm between the radius and ulna. Passing through the olecranon and along the lateral aspect of the upper arm, it reaches the shoulder region where it goes across and passes behind the Gall Bladder Meridian of Foot-Shaoyang and winding over the supraclavicular fossa, where it spreads in the chest to connect with the pericardium. It then descends through the diaphragm and down to the abdomen and joins its pertaining organ, the upper, middle and lower jiao (i. e. Sanjiao).

A branch originates from the chest (Tanzhong, RN 17). Running upward, it emerges from the supraclavicular fossa. From there it ascends to the neck. Running along the posterior border of the ear, and further to the corner of the anterior hairline and up to the forehead, then it turns downward to the cheek, and it terminates in the infraorbital region.

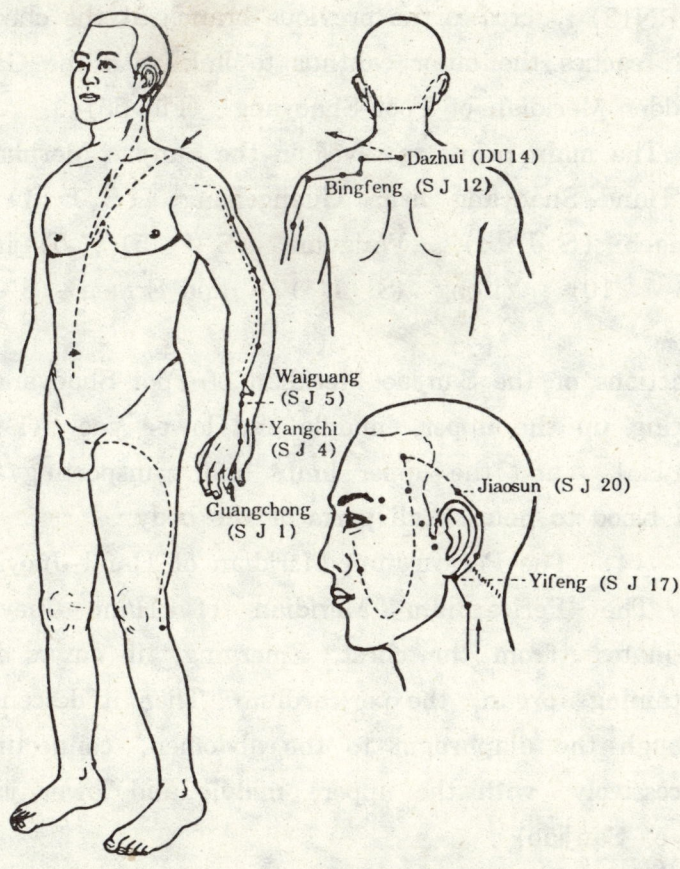

Fig. 65
The circulatory route of the Sanjiao Meridian of Hand-Shaoyang

Another branch arises from the retroauricular region and enters the ear. Then it emerges in front of the ear, passing in front of the point Shangguan

(RN13), crosses the previous branch at the cheek and reaches the outer canthus to link with the Gall Bladder Meridian of Foot-Shaoyang (Fig. 65).

The main points involved in the Sanjiao Meridian of Hand-Shaoyang are: Guangchong (S J 1), Yangchi (S J 4), Waiguan (S J 5), Tiajing (S J 10), Yifeng (S J 17) and Ermen (S J 21).

Functions of the Sanjiao Meridian of Foot-Shaoyang: linking up the upper, middle and lower jiao (i.e. Sanjiao) and the upper limbs and transporting Qi and blood to nourish all parts of the body.

(4) The Pericardium Meridian of Hand-Jueyin

The Pericardium Meridian of Hand-Jueyin originates from the chest. Emerging, it enters its pertaining organ, the pericardium. Then it descends through the diaphragm to the abdomen, connecting successively with the upper, middle and lower jiao (i.e. Sanjiao).

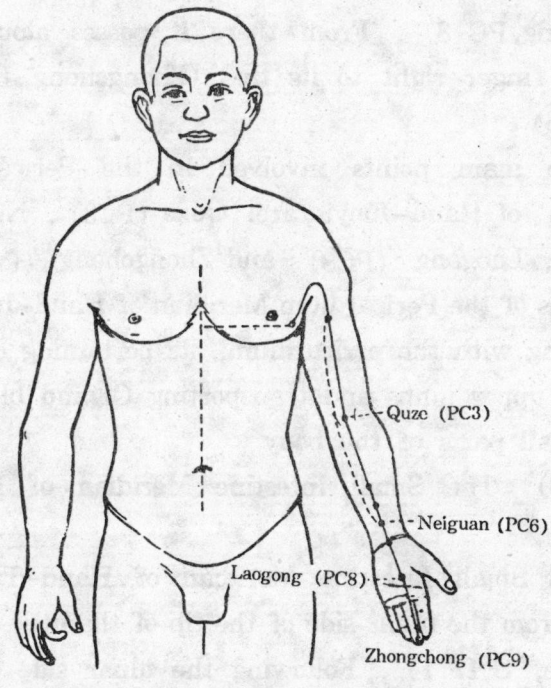

Fig. 66
The circulatory route of the Pericardium Meridian of Hand-Jueyin

A branch arising from the chest runs inside the chest, emerges from the costal region at the point Tianchi (PC1), 3 cun below the anterior axillary fold and ascends to the axilla. Following the medial aspect of the upper arm, it turns downward between the Lung Meridian of Hand-Taiyin and the Heart

Meridian of Hand-Shaoyin and enters the palm (Laogong, PC 8). From there it passes along the middle finger right to its tip (Zhongchong, PC 9) (Fig. 66).

The main points involved in the Pericardium Meridian of Hand-Jueyin are: Quze (PC3), Neiguan (PC6), Laogong (PC8) and Zhongchong (PC9). Functions of the Pericardium Meridian of Hand-Jueyin: connecting with the pericardium, its pertaining organ, and the upper limbs and transporting Qi and blood to nourish all parts of the body.

(5) The Small Intestine Meridian of Hand-Taiyang

The Small Intestine Meridian of Hand-Taiyang starts from the ulnar side of the tip of the little finger (Shaoze, S I 1). Following the ulnar side of the dorsum of the hand it reaches the wrist where it emerges from the styloid process of the ulnar. From there it ascends along the posterior aspect of the forearm, passes between the olecranon of the ulnar and the middle epicondyle of the humerus, and runs along the posterior border of the lateral aspect of the upper arm to the shoulder joint. Circling around the scapular region (Tianzong, S I 11), it meets Dazhui (DU 14) on the superior aspect of the shoulder. Then, turning downward to the supraclavicular fossa, it connects with the heart. From there it descends along the esophagus, passes through the diaphragm, reaches the stomach, and finally enters the small intestine, its pertaining organ.

The branch from the supraclavicular fossa ascends to the neck, and further to the cheek. Via the outer canthus, it enters the ear (Tinggong, S I 19).

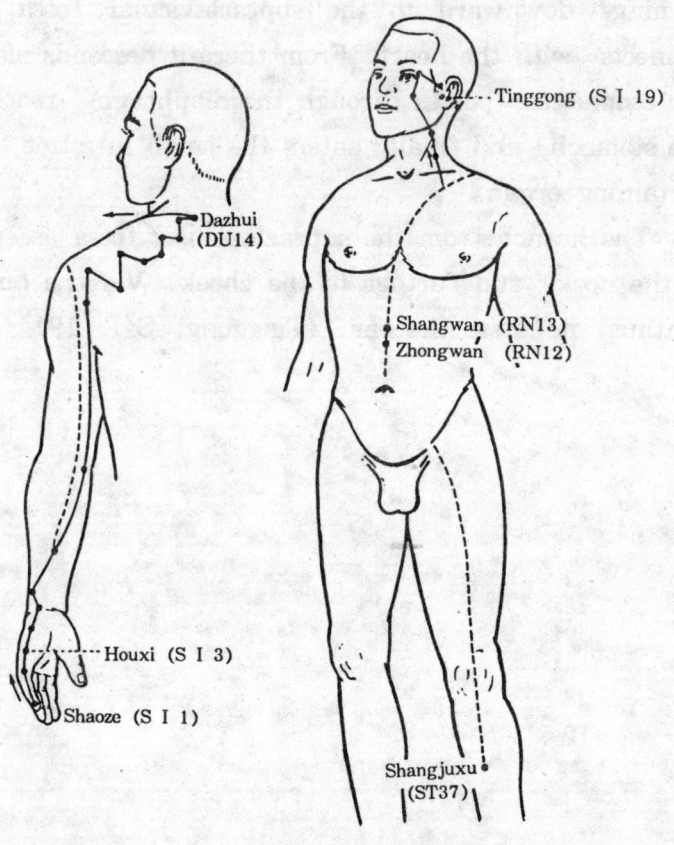

Fig. 67
The circulatory route of the Small Intestine Meridian of Hand-Taiyang

The branch from the cheek runs upward to the infraorbital region (Quanliao, S I 18) and futher to the lateral side of the nose. Then, it reaches the inner canthus (Jingming, BL 1) to link with the Urinary Bladder Meridian of Foot-Taiyang (Fig. 67).

The main points involved in the Small Intestine Meridian of Hand-Taiyang are: Shaoze (S I 1), Houxi (S I 3) and Tinggong (S I 19).

Functions of the Small Intestine Meridian of Hand-Taiyang: mainly connecting with the small intestine, its pertaining organ, and the upper limbs and transporting Qi and blood to nourish all parts of the body.

(6) The Heart Meridian of Hand-Shaoyin

The Heart Meridian of Hand-Shaoyin originates from the heart. Emerging, it spreads over the 'heart system' (i. e. the tissues connecting the heart with the other Zang-Fu organs). It passes through the diaphragm to connect with the small intestine.

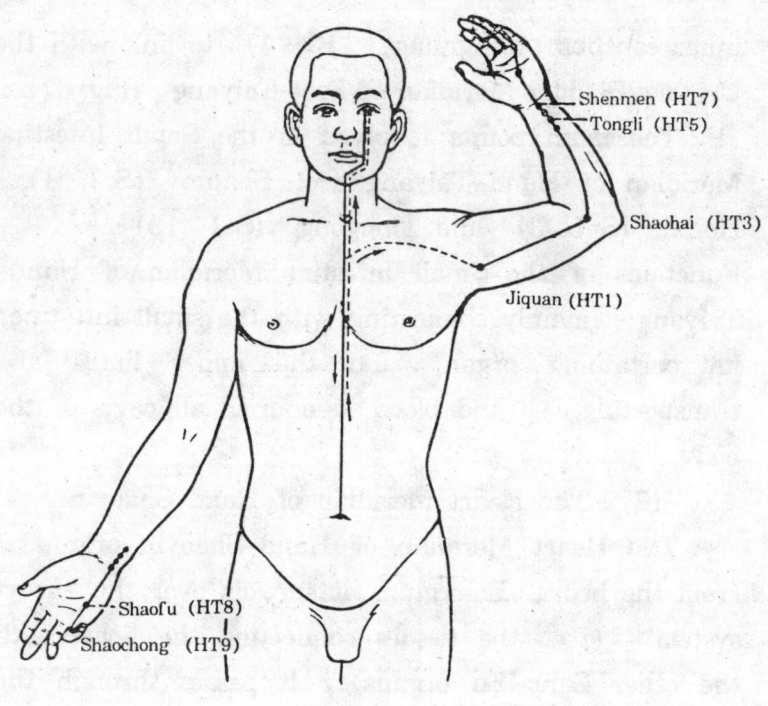

Fig. 68
The circulatory route of the Heart Meridian of Hand-Shaoyin

The straight portion of the meridian from the 'heart system' goes upward to the lung. Then, it turns downward from the axilla (Jiquan, HT1). From there it goes along the posterior border of the medial aspect of the upper arm behind the Lung Meridian of Hand-Taiyin and the Pericardium Meridian of Hand-Jueyin down to the cubital fossa.

From there it descends along the posterior border of the medial aspect of the forearm to the pisiform region proximal to the palm and enters the palm. Then, it follows the medial aspect of the little finger to its tip (Shaochong, HT9) and links with the Small Intestine Meridian of Hand-Taiyang (Fig. 68).

Main points involved in the Heart Meridian of Hand-Shaoyin are: Jiquan (HT1), Shaohai (HT3), Shenmen (HT7), Shaofu (HT8) and Shaochong (HT9).

Functions of the Heart Meridian of Hand-Shaoyin: mainly connecting with the heart and the upper limbs and transporting Qi and blood to nourish all parts of the body.

5. MERIDIANS INVOLVED IN PATTERN ZU LI QIAN KUN

The meridians involved in the pattern Zu LI Qian Kun are the three Yang and three Yin Meridians of Foot, the Yangqiao and Yinqiao Meridians and Yangwei and Yinwei Meridians.

(1) The Stomach Meridian of Foot-Yangming

The Stomach Meridian of Foot-Yangming starts from the lateral side of alanasi (Yingxing, L I 20).

It ascends to the bridge of the nose, where it meets the Urinary Bladder Meridian of Foot-Taiyang. Turning downward along the lateral side of the nose (Chenqi, ST 1), it enters the upper gum. Reemerging, it curves around the lips and descends to meet the Ren Meridian at the mentolabial groove (Chengjiang, RN 24). Then it runs posterolaterally across the lower portion of the cheek at Daying (ST5). Winding along the angle of the mandible (Jiache, ST6), it ascends in front of the ear and traverses Shangguan (GB3). Then, it follows the anterior hairline and reaches the forehead (Touwei, ST8).

The facial branch emerging in front of Daying (ST5), runs downward to Renying (ST9). From there it goes along the throat and enters the supraclavicular fossa. Descending, it passes through the diaphragm, enters the stomach, its pertaining organ, and connects with the spleen.

The straight portion of the meridian arising from the supraclavicular fossa runs downward, passing through the nipple. It descends by the umbilicus and enters Qichong (ST30) on the lateral side of the lower abdomen.

The branch from the lower orifice of the stomach descends inside of the abdomen, and joins the previous portion of the meridian at Qichong (ST30). Running downward, traversing Biguan (ST31), and further through Femur-Futu (ST32), it reaches the knee. From there, it continues downward along the anterior border of the lateral side of the tibia, passes through the dorsum of the foot, and reaches the lateral side of the tip of the 2nd toe (Lidui, ST 45).

The tibia branch emerges from Zusanli (ST36), 3 cun below the knee, and enters the lateral side of the middle toe.

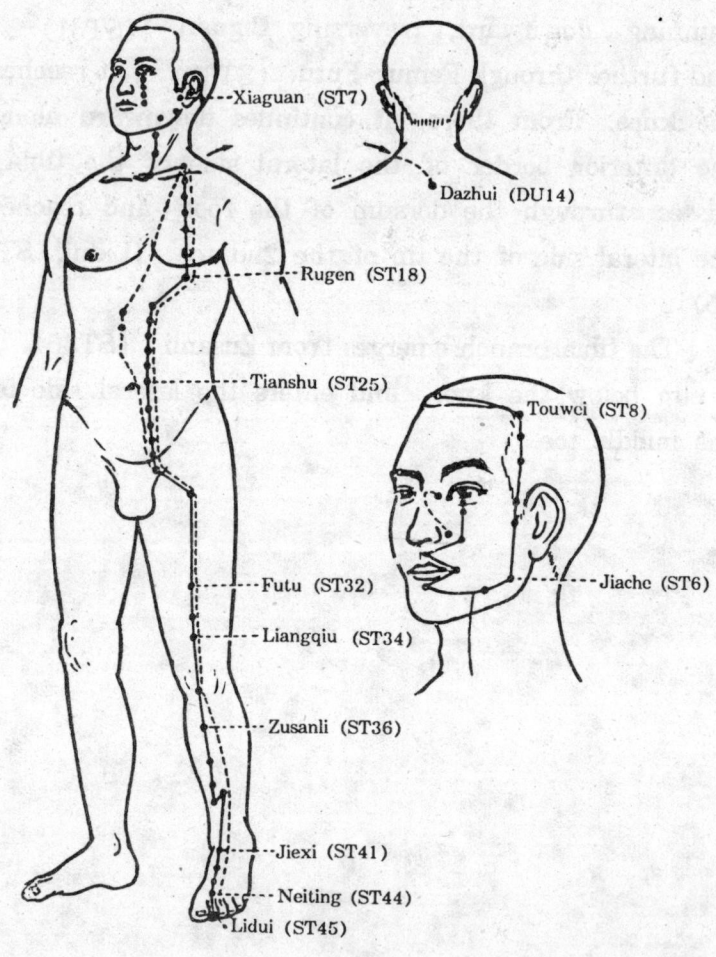

Fig. 69
The circulatory route of the Stomach Meridian of Foot-Yangming

The branch from the dorsum of the foot arises from Chongyang (ST42) and terminates at the medial side of the tip of the great toe (Yinbai, SP 1), where it links with the Spleen Meridian of Foot-Taiyin (Fig. 69).

The main points involved in the Stomach Meridian of Foot-Yangming are: Sibai (ST2), Dicang (ST 4), Jiache (ST6), Xiaguan (ST7), Touwei (ST8), Rugen (ST18), Tainshu (ST25), Futu (ST32), Liangqiu (ST34), Zusanli (ST 36), Fenglong (ST40), Jiexi (ST41), Neiting (ST44), and Lidui (ST45).

Functions of the Stomach Meridian of Foot-Yangming: mainly connecting with the stomach, its pertaining organ and the lower limbs and transporting Qi and blood to all parts of the body.

(2) The Spleen Meridian of Foot-Taiyin

The Spleen Meridian of Foot-Taiyin starts from the tip of the big toe (Yinbai, SP1). It runs along the medial aspect of the foot at the junction of the red and white skin, and ascends in front of the medial malleolus up to the medial aspect of the leg. It follows the posterior aspect of the tibia, crosses and goes in front of the Liver Meridian of Foot-Jueyin. Passing through the anterior medial aspect of the knee and

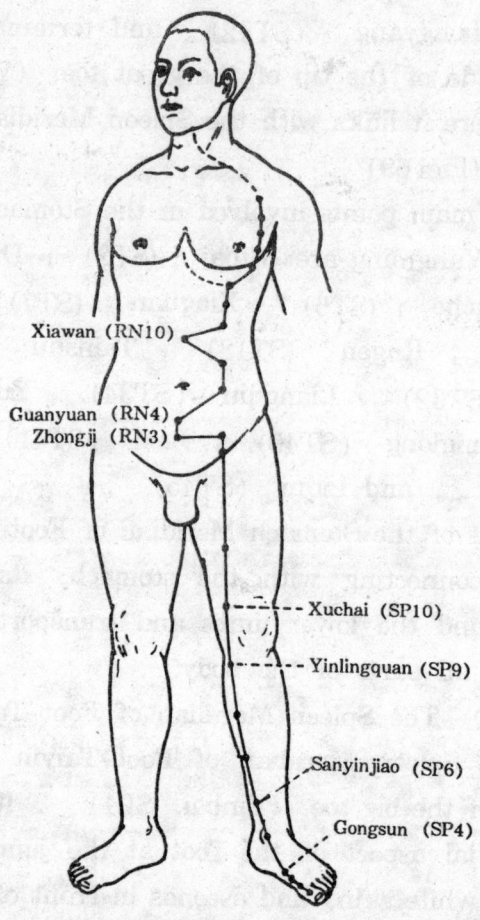

Fig. 70
The circulatory route of the Spleen Meridian of Foot-Taiyin

thigh, it enters the abdomen, then the spleen, its pertaining organ, and connects with the stomach. From there, it ascends, passing through the diaphragm and running alongside the esophagus. When it reaches the root of the tongue, it spreads over its lower surface.

The branch from the stomach goes upwards through the diaphragm, and flows into the heart to link with the Heart Meridian of Hand-Shaoyin (Fig. 70).

The main points involved in the Spleen Meridian of Foot-Taiyin are: Yinbai (SP1), Gongsun (SP 4), Sanyinjiao (SP6), Yinlinquan (SP9) and Xuehai (SP10).

Functions of the Spleen Meridian of Foot-Taiyin: mainly connecting with the spleen and the lower limbs and transporting Qi and blood to all parts of the body.

(3) The Gallbladder Meridian of Foot-Shaoyang

The Gallbladder Meridian of Foot-Shaoyang originates from the outer canthus (Tongziliao, GB 1), ascends to the corner of the forehead, then curves downward to the retroauricular region (Fengchi, (GB20) and runs along the side of the neck in front of the Sanjiao Meridian of Hand-Shaoyang to the shoulder. Turning back, it traverses and passes behind the Sanjiao Meridian of Hand-Shaoyang down to the supraclavicular fossa (Quepen, ST12) .

The retroauricular branch arises from the retroauricular region and enters the ear. It then comes out and passes the preauricular region to the posterior aspect of the outer canthus.

The branch arising from the outer canthus runs downward to Daying (ST5) and meets the Sanjiao Meridian of Hand-Shaoyang in the infraorbital region. Then, passing through Jiache (ST6), it descends to the neck and enters the supraclavicular fossa (Quepen, ST12), where it meets the main meridian. From there it further descends into the chest, passes through the diaphragm to connect with the liver and enters its pertaining organ, the Gallbladder. Then it runs inside the hypochondriac region, comes out from the lateral side of the lower abdomen near the femoral artery at the inguinal region. From there it runs superficially along the margin of the pubic hair and goes transversely into the hip region (Huantiao, GB30) .

The straight portion of the meridian runs downward from the supraclavicular fossa (Quepen, ST12), passes in front of the axilla along the lateral aspect of the chest and through the free ends of the floating ribs to the hip region where it meets the previous

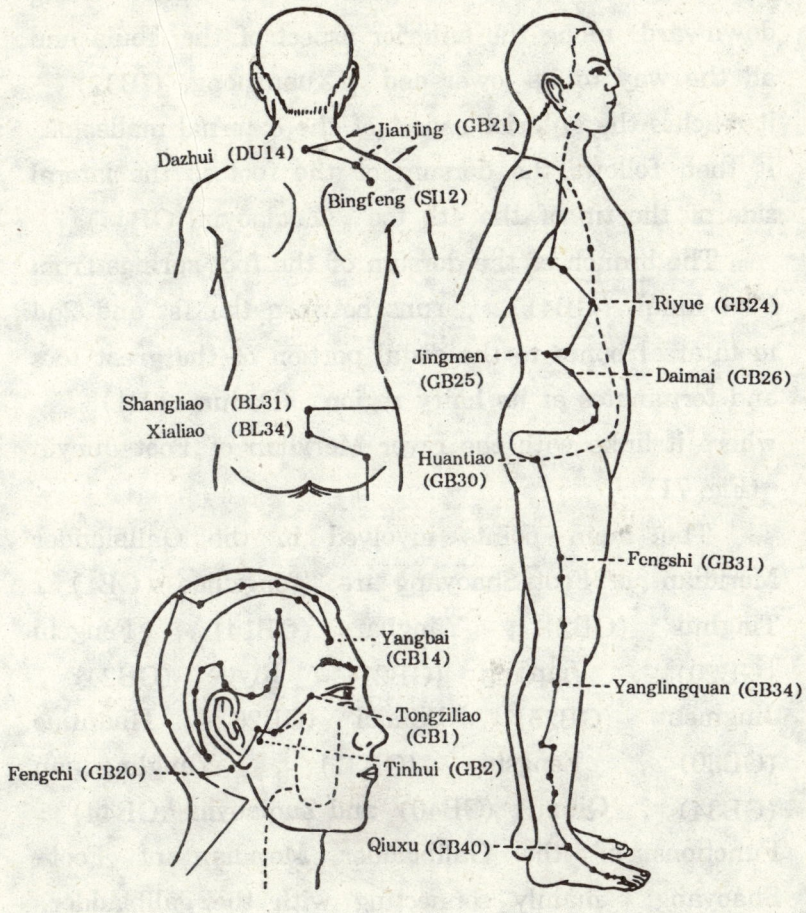

Fig. 71
The circulatory route of the Gallbladder Meridian of Foot-Shaoyang

branch. Then it descends along the lateral aspect of the thigh to the lateral side of the knee. Going downward along the anterior aspect of the fibula and all the way to its lower end (Xuanzhong, GB39), it reaches the anterior aspect of the external malleolus. It then follows the dorsum of the foot to the lateral side of the tip of the 4th toe (Zuqiaoyin, GB44).

The branch of the dorsum of the foot springs from Foot-Linqi (GB41), runs between the 1st and 2nd metatarsal bones to the distal portion of the great toes and terminates at its hairy region (Dadun, LR1), where it links with the Liver Meridian of Foot-Jueyin (Fig. 71).

The main points involved in the Gallbladder Meridian of Foot-Shaoyang are: Tongziliao (GB1), Tinghui (GB2), Yangbai (GB14), Fengchi (GB20), Jianjing (GB21), Riyue (GB24), Jingmen (GB25), Daimai (GB26), Huantiao (GB30), Fengshi (GB31), Yanglingquan (GB34), Qiuxu (GB40) and Zuqiaoyin (GB44). Functions of the Gallbladder Meridian of Foot-Shaoyang: mainly connecting with the gallbladder, its pertaining organ and the lower abdomen and transporting Qi and blood to nourish all parts of the body.

(4) The Liver Meridian of Foot-Jueyin

The Liver Meridian of Foot-Jueyin starts from the dorsal hairy region of the great toe (Dadun, LR 1). Running upward along the dorsum of the foot, passing through Zhongfeng (LR4), 1 cun in front of the medial malleolus, it ascends to an area above the medial malleolus, where it turns across and behind the Spleen Meridian of Foot-Taiyin. Then it turns further to the medial aspect of the knee and along the medial aspect of the thigh to the pubic hair region, where it curves around the external genitalia and goes up the lower abdomen. It then runs upward and curves round the stomach to enter the liver, its pertaining organ and connects with the gallbladder. From there it continues to ascend, passing through the diaphragm and branching out in the costal and hypochondriac region. Then it ascends along the posterior aspect of the throat to the nasopharynx and connects with the 'eye system'. Running upward, it emerges from the forehead and meets the Du Meridian at the vertex.

The branch arising from the 'eye system' runs downward into the cheek and curves around the inner surface of the lips.

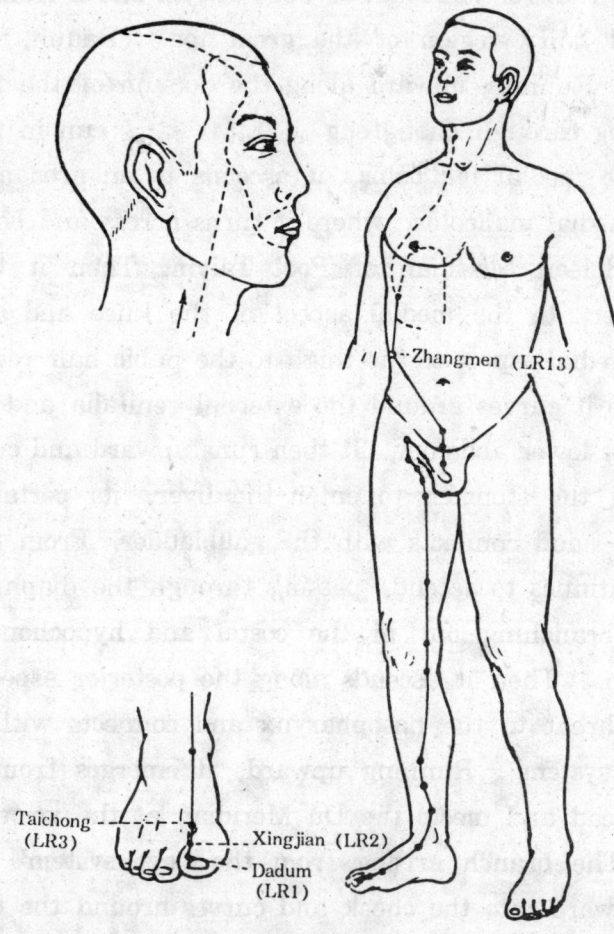

Fig. 72
The circulatory route of the Liver Meridian of Foot-Jueyin

The branch arising from the liver passes through the diaphragm, runs into the lung and links with the Lung Meridian of Hand-Taiyin (Fig. 72).

The main points involved in the Liver Meridian of Foot-Jueyin are; Dadun (LR1), Xingjian (LR2), Taichong (LR3) and Zhangmen (LR13).

Functions of the Liver Meridian of Foot-Jueyin: mainly connecting with the liver, its pertaining organ and the lower limbs and transporting Qi and blood to nourish all parts of the body.

(5) The Urinary Bladder Meridian of Foot-Taiyang

The Urinary Bladder Meridian of Foot-Taiyang starts from the inner canthus (Jingming, BL 1). Ascending to the forehead, it joins the Du Meridian at the vertex (Baihui, DU20), where a branch arises, running to the temple.

The straight portion of the meridian enters and communicates with the brain. From the vertex, it then emerges and bifurcates to descend along the posterior aspect of the neck. Running alongside the medial aspect of the scapula region and parallel to the vertebral column, it reaches the lumbar region, where it enters the body cavity via the praravertebral muscle to connect with the kidney and join its pertaining organ, the

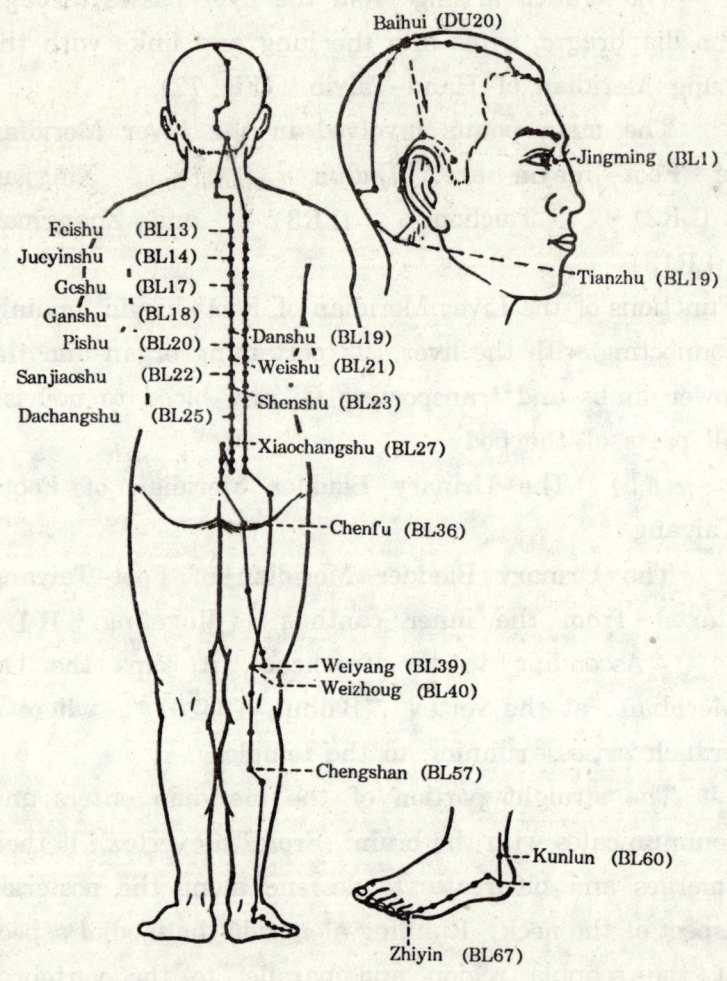

Fig. 73
The circulatory route of the Bladder Meridian of Foot- Taiyang

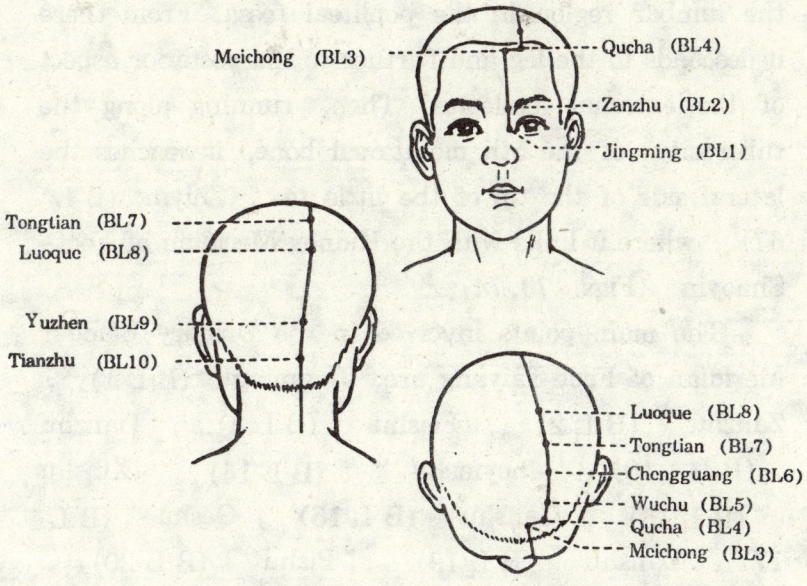

Fig. 74
The circulatory route of the Bladder Meridian of Foot-Taiyang

urinary bladder.

The branch of the lumbar region descends through the gluteal region and ends in the popliteal fossa.

The branch from the posterior aspect of the neck runs straight downward along the medial border of the scapula. Passing through the gluteal region (Huantiao, GB 30) downward along the lateral aspect of the thigh, it meets the preceding branch descending from the lumbar region in the popliteal fossa. From there it descends to the leg and further to the posterior aspect of the external malleolus. Then, running along the tuberosity of the 5th metatarsal bone, it reaches the lateral side of the tip of the little toe (Zhiyin, (B L 67), where it links with the Kidney Meridian of Foot-Shaoyin (Figs. 73, 74).

The main points involved in the Urinary Bladder Meridian of Foot-Taiyang are: Jingming (B L 1), Zanzhu (B L 2), Feishu (B L 3), Tianzhu (B L 10), Jueyinshu (B L 14), Xinshu (B L 15), Ganshu (B L 16), Geshu (B L 17), Danshu (B L 19), Pishu (B L 20), Weishu (B L 21), Sanjiaoshu (B L 22), Shenshu (B L 23), Dachangshu (B L 25), Xiaochangshu (B L 27), Pangguangshu (B L 28), Chengfu (B L 36), Weizhong (B L 40), Chengshan (B L 57), Kunlun (B L 60) and Zhiyin (B L 67).

Functions of the Urinary Bladder Meridian of Foot-Taiyang: mainly connecting with the urinary bladder, the back and the lower limbs and transporting Qi and blood to nourish all parts of the body.

(6) The Kidney Meridian of Foot-Shaoyin

The Kidney Meridian of Foot-Shaoyin starts from

the inferior aspect of the small toe and runs obliquely towards the sole (Yongquan, KI1) . Emerging from the lower aspect of the tuberosity of the navicular bone and running behind the medial malleolus, it enters the heel. Then ascends along the medial side of the leg to the medial side of the popliteal fossa and goes further upward along the posteromedial aspect of the thigh towards the vertebral column (Chengqiang, DU1) , where it enters the Kidney, its pertaining organ, and connects with the urinary bladder.

The straight portion of the meridian reemerges from the kidney. Ascending and passing through the liver and diaphragm, it enters the lung, runs along the throat and terminates at the root of the tongue.

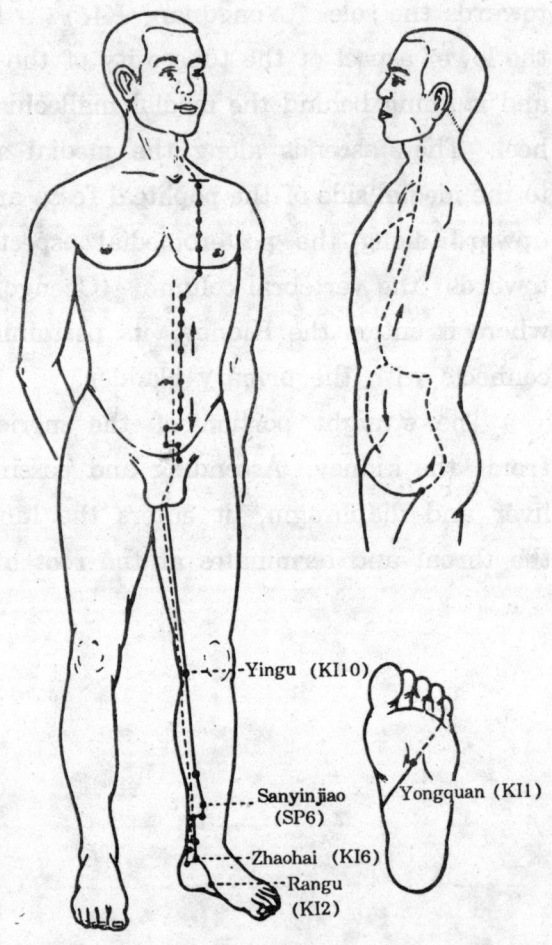

Fig. 75
The circulatory route of the Kidney Meridian of Foot-Shaoyin

A branch springs from the lung, joins the heart and runs into the chest to link with the Pericardium Meridian of Hand-Jueyin (Fig. 75).

The main points involved in the Kidney Meridian of Foot-Shaoyin are: Yongquan (KI1), Rangu (KI2), Taixi (KI3), Zhaohai (KI6) and Yingu (KI10). Functions of the Kidney Meridian of Foot-Shaoyin: mainly linking with the kidney, its pertaining organ, and the lower limbs and transporting Qi and blood to nourish all parts of the body.

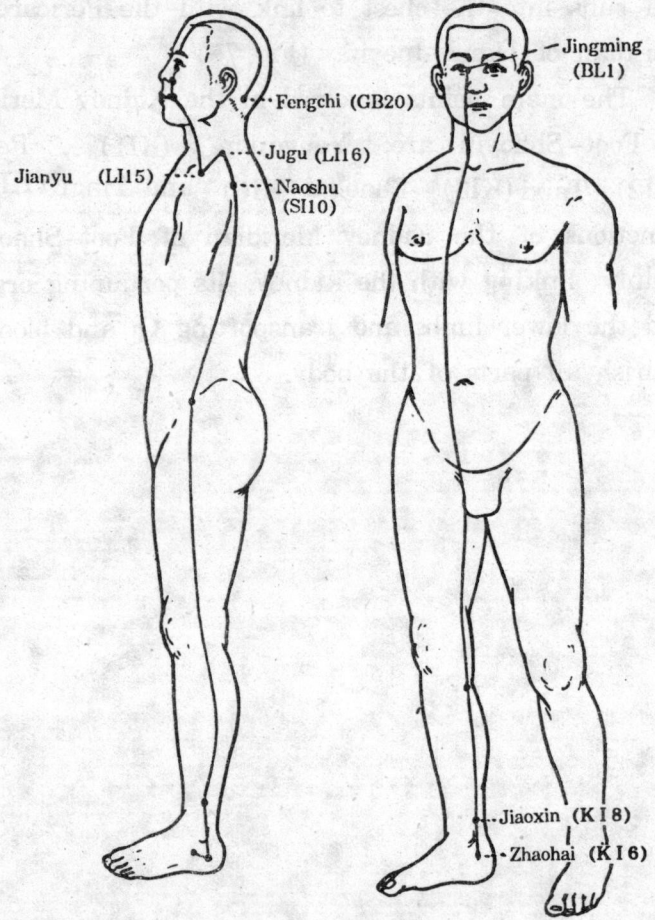

Fig. 76
The circulatory routes of the Yangqiao and Yinqiao Meridians

(7) Yangqiao Meridian

The Yangqiao Meridian starts from the lateral side of the heel (Pushen, B L 61) (Shenmai, B L 62). It runs upward along the external malleolus and passes the posterior border of the fibula, it then goes onwards along the lateral side of the thigh and posterior side of the hypochondrium to the posterior axilllary fold. From there, it winds over to the shoulder and ascends along the neck to the corner of the mouth. Then it enters the inner canthus (Jingming, B L 1) to communicate with the Yinqiao Meridian. Running further upward along the Urinary Bladder Meridian of Foot-Taiyang to the forehead, it meets the Gallbladder Meridian of Foot-Shaoyang at Fengchi (GB20) (Fig. 76).

The coalescent points of the Yangqiao Meridian are: Shenmai (B L 62), Pushen (B L 61), Fuyang (B L 59), Femur-Juliao (GB29), Naoshu (S I 10), Jianyu (L I 15), Jugu (L I 16), Tianliao (S J 15), Dichang (ST 4), Nose-Juliao (ST3), Chenqi (ST1), Jingming (B L 1) and Fengchi (GB20).

(8) Yinqiao Meridian

The Yinqiao Meridian starts from the posterior aspect of the navicular bone (Zhaohai, KI 6). Ascending to the upper portion of the medial malleolus, it runs straight upward along tho posterior border of the medial aspect of the thigh to the external genitalia. Then it goes upward along the chest to the supraclavicular fossa and runs further upward laterally to the Adam's apple in front of the Renying (ST9) and then along the zygoma. From there, it reaches the inner canthus (Jingming, B L 1) and communicates with the Yangqiao Meridian (Fig. 76).

The coalescent points of the Yinqiao Meridian are: Zhaohai (KI6), Jiaoxin (KI8), and Jingming (B L 1).
Functions of the Yangqiao and the Yinqiao Meridians: working together to coordinate the movements of the four limbs and the opening-closing function of the eyelids.

On one hand, the word 'qiao' in Chinese bears the meaning 'the heel of the foot' and 'nimble'. The names 'Yangqiao' and 'Yinqiao' Meridians suggest that these two meridians perform the functions of making the lower limbs dexterous and quick in action. The Yangqiao and Yinqiao Meridians run upward to the head respectively along the lateral and medial aspect of the lower limbs. They have the functions of linking up the meridian energy of the

Yin and Yang meridians all over the body and regulating the movements of the four limbs. That is why they can make the lower limbs dexterous and quick in action. On the other hand, the Yangqiao and Yinqiao Meridians communicate with each other in the inner canthus (Jingming, B L 1) and enter the brain, their pertaining organ. That is why they can regulate the opening-closing function of the eyelids.

The medical classics "Miraculous Pivot-Cold and Fever" says "If Yang Qi is excessive, the eyes are apt to stay wide open; if Yin Qi is excessive, the eyes are inclined to close". That is, when Wei Qi (defensive energy) abnormally circulates in Yangqiao Meridian, the functions of the Yangqiao Meridian become so vigorous that the eyes are kept wide open all the time and one feels it difficult to fall asleep; when the Wei Qi abnormally circulates in Yinqiao Meridian, the functions of Yinqiao become vigorous and as a result, one will become so sleepy and tired and the eyes are inclined to close. The Chapter "Pulse Conditions" in the Classics "Miraculous Pivot" says, "In males, the Yangqiao Meridian functions as a motive force and plays a leading role, so males are relatively more active; while in females, the Yinqiao Meridian's function is more vigorous than that of the Yangqiao

Meridian, therefore, females are less active or indolent. "What have been mentioned above shows that the functions of the Yangqiao and Yinqiao Meridians have an important bearing on human body's activities and sleep.

The practice of this pattern can, therefore, reinforce the circulation of the Defensive Qi through the Yangqiao and Yinqiao Meridians.

(9) Yangwei Meridian

The Yangwei Meridian originates from the heel (Jinmen, B L 63) and emerges from the external malleolus. Ascending along the Gallbladder Meridian of Foot-Shaoyang, it passes through the hip region. Then it runs further upward along the posterior aspect of the hypochondriac and costal region and the posterior aspect of the axilla to the shoulder and to the forehead. It then turns backward to the back of the neck, where it communicates with the Du Meridian (Fengfu, DU 16, Yamen, DU15) (Fig. 77).

The coalescent points of the Yangwei Meridian are: Jinmen (B L 63), Yangjiao (GB35), Naoshu (S I 10), Tianliao (S J 15), Jianjing (GB16), Touwei (S J 8), Benshen (G B 13), Yangbai (GB14), Toulinqi (GB15), Muchuang (GB16), Zhengying (GB17), Chengling (GB18),

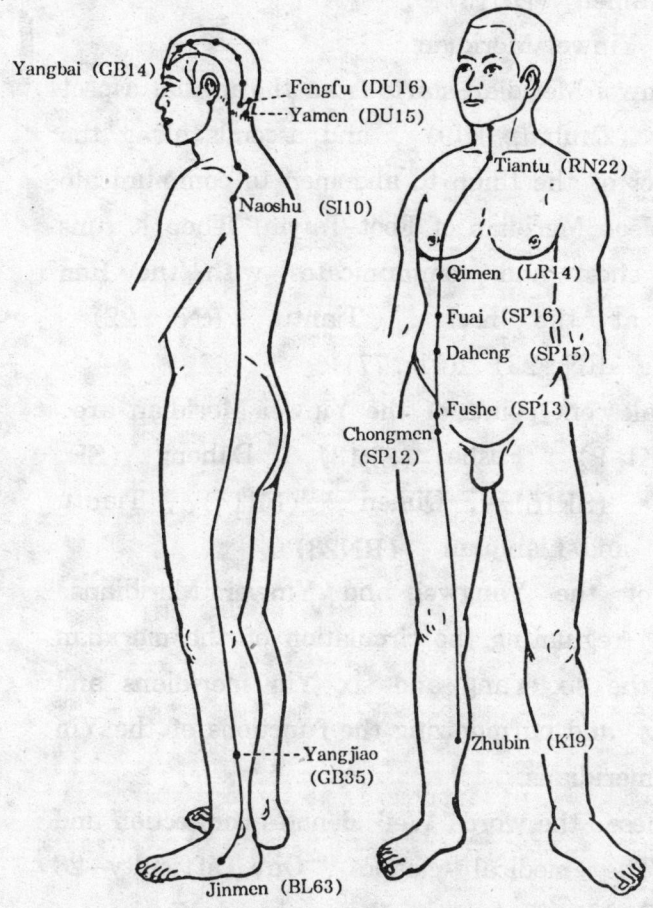

Fig. 77
The circulatory routes of the Yangwei and Yinwei Meridians

Naokong (GB19) , Fengchi (GB20) , Fengfu (DU 16) and Yamen (DU15) .

(10) Yinwei Meridian

The Yinwei Meridian starts from the medial aspect of the leg (Zhubin, KI9) , and ascends along the medial aspect of the thigh to abdomen to communicate with the Spleen Meridian of Foot-Taiyin. Then it runs along the chest and communicates with the Ren Meridian at the neck (Tiantu, RN 22) , (Lianquan, RN 23) (Fig. 77) .

The coalescent points of the Yinwei Meridian are: Zhubin (KI 9) , Fushe (SP13) , Daheng (SP 15) , Fuai (SP16) , Qimen (LR14) , Tiantu (RN22) and Lianquan (RN23) .

Functions of the Yangwei and Yinwei Meridians: respectively regulating the circulation of the meridian energy of the six Yang and six Yin meridians and coordinating and harmonizing the functions of the Yin and Yang meridians.

In Chinese, the word 'Wei' denotes connection and network. The medical classics " On Difficulty- 28 Difficult Problems" says, " Yangwei and Yinwei are meridians connecting with meridians of the whole body and maintaining the bodily functions. Instead of serving as streams transporting Qi and blood, these two meridians function as lakes to store the overflowing Qi and blood of the other meridians". This means that the Yangwei has the functions of maintaining and connecting with the Yang meridians of the whole body and the Yinwei Meridian has the functions of maintaining and connecting with the Yin meridians of the whole body. The former, linking up the Yang meridians, dominates the exterior of the whole body and communicates with the Du Meridian at points Fengchi (DU16) and Yamen (DU15) : while the latter, linking up the Yin meridians of the whole body, dominates the interior of the whole body and communicates with the Ren Meridian at points Tiantu (RN22) and Lianquan (RN23) . Normally, the Yinwei and Yangwei Meridians connect with each other and together play a role in regulating the circulation of Qi and blood of the whole body and storing the overflowing Qi and blood and letting them out to the meridians in case of insufficiency. However, they do not join the other meridians in their circulation. In case of functional disorders and appearance of corresponding disease symptoms, the practice of this Qigong pattern is likely to relieve them.

6. MERIDIAN INVOLVED IN PATTERN JIA YAO YU DAI

The meridian involved in this pattern is the Dai Meridian. The Dai Meridian originates below the hypochondriac region and runs obliquely downward through Daimai (GB26), Wushu (GB27) and Weidao (GB28). It runs transversely around the waist like a girdle (Fig. 78).

The coalescent points of the Dai Meridian are: Daimai (GB26), Wushu (GB27) and Weidao (GB28).

Functions of the Dai Meridian: the word 'Dai' in Chinese denotes a girdle or belt. As this meridian runs transversely around the waist and binds up all the longitudinal meridians, it is called Dai Meridian. As is suggested in the name, the Dai Meridian mainly has the function of controlling all the meridians. Starting from the second lumbar vertebra and running around the waist, it keeps all the Yin and Yang meridians under its control. Besides, as it emerges from the Du Meridian and circles round the waist where the meridian energy of the Chong, Ren and Du Meridian originate (these three meridians all originate from the uterus),

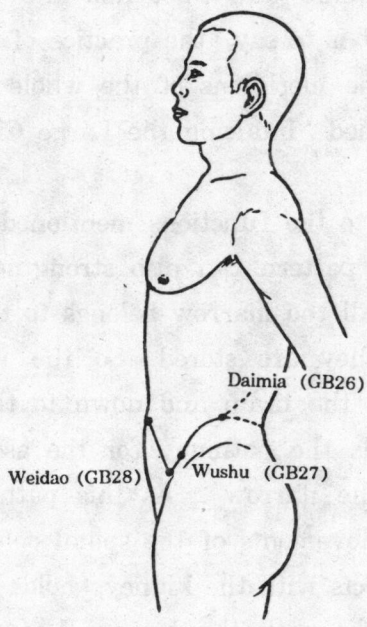

Fig. 78
The circulatory route of the Dai Meridian

the Dai Meridian has a very close relationship with these three meridians.

7. MERIDIANS INVOLVED IN PATTERN YUN ZHUAN QIAN KUN

The meridians involved in this pattern are the three Yang Meridians of Hand and Foot, the three Yin

Meridians of Hand and Foot and the Eight Extra Meridians, that is to say, the practice of this pattern acts upon all the meridians of the whole body. That is why it is named 'Inducing the Large Circulation of Qi'.

In addition to the functions mentioned above, the practice of this pattern can also strengthen the 'Sea of Marrow'. "All the marrow belongs to the brain no matter where they are stored. So the whole spinal column, up to the brain and down to the coccygeal region, serves as the pathmay for the ascending and descending of the narrow". As this pattern involves wide range of movements of the spinal colum, which, in a way, connects with the kidney, holds the marrow and communicates with the brain. Frequent practice of this pattern can make the practitioners more energetic and vigorous.

8. FUNCTION OF THE PATTERN WU QI CHAO YUAN

Exerting the same effects on the meridians all over the body as the above patterns do, this pattern mainly aims at concentrating into Dantian the Yuan Qi (primordial energy) of the five Zang organs which has already been stimulated and mobilized by the previous seven patterns and the Qi of the universe (from the east, south, west, north and the middle).

9. FUNCTION OF THE PATTERN JIU JIU GUI ZHEN

The pattern 'Jiu Jiu Gui Zhen' has the function of guiding and inducing the meridian energy of the whole body. But it mainly aims at reinforcing the mobilized True Qi and storing in Dantian the Qi of the nature drawn into the body with the effect of the mind-concentration and imagination.
Perseverance in practising Qigong will, in the end, make the True Qi and the Qi of the nature accumulated and condensed into 'Qi elixir' or 'elixir of life'.

Appendant Table 2

Summing-up of the meridians involved in the motioned Qigong Pattern series JIU ZHUAN DA YUN TIAN

Name of the Pattern	Meridians Involved or Functions of the Pattern
HUN DUN CU KAI	opening up the points Tanzhong (RN17) and Dazhui (DU14) and then the Ren Meridian and Du Meridian
YIN YANG ER QI	the Ren and Du Meridians (Inducing the Small Circulation of Qi)
QING TIAN YI ZHU	the Chong Meridian
SHOU FEN YIN YANG	the three Yin and three Yang Meridians of Hand
ZU LI QIAN KUN	the three Yin and three Yang Meridians of Foot; the Yangqiao, Yinqiao, Yangwei and Yinwei Meridians
JIA YAO YU DAI	the Dai Meridian
YUN ZHUAN QIAN KUN	the 'Sea of Marrow', the Fourteen Regular Meridians and the Ren and Du Meridians
WU QI CHAO YUAN	conducting Yuan Qi (primordial energy) of the five Zang organs to return to Dantian
JIU JIU GUI ZHEN	reinforcing the mobilized Qi in Dantian

APPENDICES

1. Effects of Qigong 'Waiqi' in Electrophysiology

By Zhang Jin Mei et al.
Department of Physiology, Sun Yat-Sen
University of Medical Sciences, Guangzhou
Chen Yan Feng et al.
Guangdong Qigong Research Association

Qigong is one of the precious legacies of Traditional Chinese Medicine. The Qigong Research Coordinating Group in Sun Yat-sen University of Medical Sciences has studied the biological effects and mechanism in Qigong 'Waiqi' by means of modern techniques. The initial report is as follows:

Among the 25 spontaneous unit discharges of the rats vermian cells, 23 were alternated after receiving 'Waiqi' released by Qigong masters. The effect rate was up to 92%. The spontaneous unit discharges of the cells were affected by the control of the Qigong masters thought. Under the control of the masters thought, 6 spontaneous unit discharges were increased when stimulated; 5 were decreased when inhibited; 9 were made to increase when stimulated by the concentrated-mind of the Qigong masters and decrease when inhibited; 3 spontaneous unit discharges, while stimulated by Qigong masters' concentrated-minds, were decreased instead of being increased. There was no alternation in the spontaneous unit discharges when the vermian cells received 'Waiqi' mimiced by ordinary people.

Experiments also showed that prior to receiving 'Waiqi' released by Qigong masters, the RP (rest potential) of transmembrane of the papillary muscles in the right ventricle of the guinea pig was -97.8 ± 0.6mV ($X \pm SE$, $n = 18$); the APA (action potential amplitude) of the transmembrane potential was 134.6 ± 0.7mV; the ERP (effective refractory period) of transmembrane potential was 186 ± 3.9mS; the APD_{90} of the transmembrane potential (action potential duration, the time when transmembrane potential repolarized up to 90% from the top) was 179.6 ± 6.4mS. The parameters reduced or shortened by 2.4%, 2.2%, 2.0% and 1.6% respectively after receiving 'Waiqi' for fifteen minutes. There showed in the above data an obvious statistically significant difference. While the mimiced 'Waiqi' released by ordinary people was of no significance in statistics.

The above results suggested that Qigong 'Waiqi' can alternate the spontaneous unit discharges of the cerebellar cells in rats and can change every parameter of the transmembrane potential of the papillary muscles of the right ventricle in guinea pig. Further approaches to the mechanism of Qigong 'Waiqi' are needed.

2. Improvement in Visual Acuity and Increase in Vital Capacity by Practising the Prenatal Energy Mobilizing Qigong

By Xiao Xin He
Ke Heng et al.
Guangdong Qigong Rescarch Association

In order to investigate whether this Qigong can treat myopia and increase the vital capacity or not, our Qigong Research Office gave lectures of this Qigong to the freshmen and foreign students of Grade 87 in September, 1987. The results were satisfactory. They are classified as follows:

(1) General Data

Students totalled 33. Among them, 28 were freshmen (male, 18 and female, 10) and 5, male foreign students. The average age was 18.9. Of them 23 suffered from myopia, which accounted for 70%, and the rest 10 with normal visual acuity, which took up 30%.

(2) Qigong Patterns Practised

'Nine Patterns for Inducing the Large Circulation of Qi' of the Motioned Qigong Pattern Series was lectured, namely, HUN DUN CU KAI, YIN YANG ER QI, QING TIAN YI ZHU, SHOU FEN YIN YANG, ZU LI QIAN KUN, JIA YAO YU DAI, YUN ZHUAN QIAN KUN, WU QI CHAO YUAN, JIU JIU QUI ZHEN and the General Ending Pattern.

As for the Quiescent Qigong Pattern Series, the patterns; ' Dan-ming Breathing', and ' Interior Revolution of Qi in Dantian' had been taught, but the students were required to practise the former only.

(3) Teaching methods

We spent three hours for lecturing the Motioned Qigong Pattern Series and the Quiescent Qigong Pattern

Series including one hour each day from 4:30 to 5:30p.m. from 15th to 17th, September. Students' self-practice started from 18th, September to 11th, October, for 24 days. Every morning the students, guided by the lecturer, practised mind-tranquillization before practising Qigong. Every afternoon when students practised the Motioned Qigong Pattern Series, the lecturers would help them along and rectify their incorrect movements and gestures. After the Ending Pattern was finished, the lecturers would answer the questions from the students.

(4) Time Table for Qigong Practice

Motioned Qigong was practised 20 minutes every day from 6:30 to 6:50 a.m. and 4:30 to 4:50p.m.. In the afternoon was the practice of Motioned Qigong, then followed by a twenty-minute lecture to allow an interval of transition, rest and lecture for students to shift from the practice of Motioned Qigong to the Quiescent Qigong. Following the lecture there was a fifteen-minute practice of the Quiescent Qigong Pattern Series from 5:10 to 5:25 p.m.. The time of everyday Qigong practice totalled fifty-five minutes. The Qigong practice lasted 27 days.

(5) Methods for Examining Visual Acuity

Visual acuity tests were performed among 33

participants in Qigong practice with or without myopia, before and after the practice of Qigong in the same place with the same illimination and an international visual acuity test chart. At the same time, tests for vital capacity were also performed before and after practice. Data are shown in the enclosed chart (Table 3).

(6) Discussion

1) Among 33 students participating in the visual acuity test, 23 suffered from myopia of different degrees. The visual acuity of their left eyes totalled 8.9 and the right eyes 8.7 before practising Qigong. After twenty-seven days' Qigong practice, the total of visual acuity was increased to 12.8 for the left and 12.0 for the right, with an average increase of 0.17 and 0.14 respectively.

The table shows that 95.5% of the practitioners with myopia were improved in vision. A marked example was Zhao Huang-jian, a Korean student. The visual acuity of his left eye raised from 0.3 to 1.0 and that of his the right eye from 0.5 to 1.2. He said happily, "I can read without spectacles now!" He practised Qigong very hard and his mind was well-tranquillized in practice. He practised three times, totalled sixty minutes every day. His vital capacity was also increased from 3,500 ml to 4,000 ml and the symptoms of chronic appendicitis were relieved after a period of Qigong practice.

2) Measurements of vital capacity of the 31 students were taken before and after the practice of Qigong. It totalled 91,000ml before practice and 92,300ml after practice. There was an increase of 1,300ml. The average increase was 62ml per person.

(7) Conclusion

Though the Prenatal Energy Mobilizing Qigong is not a Qigong remedy with special effects for the treatment of myopia, after practising it, students' visual acuity was improved and their vital capacity increased and the pulmonary functions strengthened. These evidences proved that the practice of Prenatal Energy Mobilizing Qigong indeed has the function of strengthening the body and benefiting the development of intelligence.

Appendant Table 3

Comparison of Visual Acuity and Vital Capacity Among 33 Students after Practising the Prenatal Energy Mobilizing Qigong for 27 Days

Items Name	Data		Visual Acuity				Vital Capacity		Total Time of Practice (minutes)	Tranquilization of Mind
			before practice		after paractice		before practice	after practice		
			left	right	left	right	ml	ml		
Yan Jin	m	18	1.5	1.5	1.5	1.5	2750	3100	1170	good
Cai Yidong	m	18	0.2	0.2	0.2	0.2	2600	2800	1310	good
Li Jianshong	m	20	1.5	1.5	1.5	1.5	3250	3500	1150	good
Li Feiteng	m	20	0.4	0.7	1.2	0.7	2750	2100	1070	fair
Chen Xueyun	f	19	0.2	0.2	0.5	0.5	3000	3000	1250	good
Huang Xuewu	m	17	0.3	0.3	0.3	0.4	3200	3000	1290	fair
Qi Yanping	f	17	0.3	0.4	0.3	0.4	2300	2300	1350	good
Wang Haihong	f	18	1.5	1.5	1.5	1.5	2000	2000	1290	good
Li Zhongwei	m	18	1.5	1.5	1.5	1.2	3300	3300	1310	good
Xie Meihua	f	21	0.4	0.3	0.5	0.6	2250	2750	1230	fair
Liu Yaming	f	18	0.2	0.2	0.3	0.4	2000	2250	1290	good
Chen Yongyuan	m	18	0.2	0.3	0.3	0.4	3100	3800	1250	good
Jia Xiaolin	f	18	0.6	0.4	0.6	0.4	2400	2750	1330	good
Li Xueshan	m	19	1.5	1.5	1.5	1.5	2500	2800	1150	good
Zheng Zuozhong	m	18	0.3	0.3	0.5	0.3			1250	fair
Hou Jie	f	19	0.2	0.2	0.3	0.4	2000	2000	1270	good
Xu Ping	m	18	0.5	0.3	0.8	0.8	3150	3100	1290	good
Qi Yingxin	f	18	1.0	1.0	1.0	1.0	1750	2000	1250	fair
Deng Wei	m	18	0.3	0.3	0.4	0.4	3100	3400	1330	excellent
He Wenzhong	m	18	0.1	0.2	0.1	0.1	4150	3800	1190	fair
Liu Cen	m	18	0.2	0.3	0.4	0.5	3000	3000	1230	good
He Gang	m	19	0.2	0.3	0.2	0.3	3000	3000	1330	fair
Chen Wei	m	18	0.3	0.3	0.3	0.2	3250	3250	1330	good
Huang Feiping	m	20	1.5	1.5	1.5	1.5	2900	3100	1150	good
Liu Dongyang	m	18	1.5	1.5	1.5	1.5	3350	3400	1350	excellent
Li Lin	m	18	0.6	0.5	0.6	0.6	3650	3600	1230	good
Fan Xinhua	f	18	1.2	0.4	1.5	0.5			1290	fair
Zhou Xin	f	18	0.7	0.08	1.0	0.2	2000	2400	1310	good
Jin Chengzhe	m	22	1.5	1.5	1.5	1.5	4000	3800	1270	good
Zhao Huangjian	m	22	0.3	0.5	1.0	1.2	3500	4000	1290	excellent
Jin Jinshan	m	21	1.5	1.5	1.5	1.5	2600	2500	1270	good
Yang Guangri	m	22	1.5	1.5	1.5	1.5	3200	3800	1250	good
Tang Haifeng	m	22	0.3	0.3	0.5	0.3	3200	2600	1170	good

3. Recurrence of the Specific Effects of Qigong 'Waiqi' on Isolated Culture of Heart Muscle Cells

By Luo Chi Biao
Department of Biology, Jinan University

Qigong 'Waqi', which has long been used to treat diseases, glitters like a pearl in the treasury of traditional Chinese medicine. There are two tendencies in our country in its scientific investigation of the material foundation. One is the physical measurement of its objective material attribution; the other is the biomedical measurement of its biological effects.

Experiments were made in the heart muscle cell clusters with spontaneous irrhythmic pulsation chosen from the rat's ventricular muscle cells in isolated culture. The microscopical picture signals were monitored with our self-made Pattern 811 photoelectric amplifier and the curve diagram of the pulsation of the heart muscle cell clusters was recorded with an electrophysiological apparatus. The purpose of the experiment was to measure the existence of Qigong ' Waiqi' and the recurrence of its specific effects on the throbbing heart muscle cells. Ninety cell clusters were monitored and the continuous recording took 3422 minutes. 'Waiqi' was released by Qigong masters Ke Heng, Xu Jianping and Wu Yucan with Quiescent Qigong and Motioned Qigong to the heart muscle cell specimen. The results of the experiment are as follows:

(1) There were no responses observed when mimiced 'Waiqi' was given by ordinary people to the 36 cell clusters with spontaneous irrhythmic pulsation.

(2) There were marked specific effects on spontaneous irrhythmic pulsation in 54 cell clusters which received 'Waiqi' from Qigong masters. Of them, 29 were of regular rhythmic type, which accounted for 53.7%; 15 were of excitatory type, which accounted for 27.8%; 10 were of inhibitory type, which took up 18.5%.

(3) Different Qigong masters 'Waiqi' released with Quiescent and Motioned Qigong caused different pulsation responses in the same cell clusters. Master Xu's 'Waiqi' released with Quiescent Qigong had the effect of regulating the rhythmic radiation and elevating the magnitude of pulsation; while Master Ke's and Master Wu's 'Waiqi' released with Motioned Qigong had the effect of frequency-disturbing and elevating the magnitude of pulsation.

(4) Different pulsation reponses were caused in the same cell cluster by the same master's 'Waiqi' released with different Qigong patterns, Quiescent or Motioned. Generally speaking, the 'Waiqi' released with Motioned Qigong had an strong inhibition effect.

(5) When the effect of frequency-disturbing or strong inhibition was over, a normal physiological effect with regular rhythm and elevating magnitude of pulsation followed. It appeared as a negative inductivity.

Discussion: It has been observed and measured through the experiments that the 'Waiqi' released with Quiescent Qigong can inhibit the heart beats and increase the magnitude of the pulsation simultaneously, namely, it activates heart beats by increasing the pulsation rate, which is of active significance in maintaining normal physiological activities. Though, the 'Waiqi' released with Motioned Qigong disturbs the even pulsatory rhythm, it induces the heart muscle cells to beat steadily in a medium magnitude to compensate a sharp reduction in frequency. It finally reaches a new point of balance to form a fast response to the stimulation from the external environment. This might have certain physiological significance in emergency.

4. A Study of the Phenomenon of Film Sensitization by Qigong 'Waiqi'

By Zeng Xiachu et al.
Guangdong Qigong Research Association

(1) Introduction

In recent years, information on carriage of infrared radiation, static electric field, magnetic field and microparticle beam modulated by low frequency fluctuation have been picked up from Qigong 'Waiqi'. Measurement of 'Waiqi' was taken by means of gamma-ray scintillation detector, plastic scintillation detector, semiconductor detector and X-ray analyzer. But no gamma-ray and X-ray were detected. In the other aspect, whether there exist some other messages with the properties of other radiating beam in 'Waiqi' is still a question. Here, we used the film-experiment method, the most fundamental and simplest experimental means in nuclear physical research, in our experiment.

(2) Experimental Method

In the experiment, we used Gongyuan 120BW films

and its developing agent and processing bath. Packing materials were chosen as black-ink cases (thickness 2.46mm, made of polyacrylate and fillings) and black-paper bags (made of black paper, thickness 0.136mm). All packing materials were checked with intense light. No light-transmitting defects such as pinholes were found with naked eyes. The films were packed under the condition of total darkness.

(3) Results of the Experiments

Experiments were carried out separately for experimental groups and control groups. In the course of the experiments, the acupuncture points of the Qigong Masters were in contact with the black-ink-case packing but out of contact with the black-paper-bag packing, in which a plastic frame was used to press the edge of the bags. On the other hand, as stated by the Qigong masters, 'Waiqi' can penetrate the packing materials. The experimental records are shown in Table 2.

According to the results in Table 2, the detecting probabilities for the occurrences of sensitized spots in the films packed with black-ink cases and black-paper bags can be calculated as follows;

For black-ink-case packing:

$$p = \frac{n}{N} \cdot \frac{100}{100} = \frac{3}{93} \cdot \frac{100}{100} = 3.2\%$$

For balck-paper-bag packing:
$$p = \frac{n}{N} \cdot \frac{100}{100} = \frac{3}{19} \cdot \frac{100}{100} = 15.7\%$$

Notes: p——detecting probabilities
n——times of occurrence of sensitizing effect
N——times of experiment

For the control groups, four sets of experiments were carried out and are described as follows:

(A) In order to rule out the factor of spots caused by bad quality of the films, in a dark room, we took the films out of the original packing cases and developed them immediately after unpacking, which totalled 84 sheets in size of 5cm X 5cm. No sensitized spot was found in all of them.

(B) In order to find out if there was sensitizing effect on the packed films by ordinary people, we asked four persons who did not practise Qigong to mimic Qigong masters' state of emitting Qi, that is, to emit Qi imaginarily toward the films, totalling 24 sheets, from their points Laogong (PC8) and the sword-fingers (i. e. the index and the middle fingers) for 5 munutes each sheet. No sensitized spot was found in all the films.

(C) To make a comparison of our results with laser's sensitizing effect on the films under the same condition, we did a control experiment with laser, in which 3 sheets of films packed in black-ink cases were put 150cm away from the He-Ne laser (20mw output), and were irradiated respectively by laser for 5 minutes. No spot-sensitization was found.

(D) To examine the reliability of the packing methods in the experiments, we also carried out experiments to compare the sensitizing effects of sunlight radiation and in-door condition storage: a) Put films packed with black-ink cases under the radiation of the sunlight for 60 minutes. No sensitizing effect was detected. b) Let 2 sheets of films, packed with black-paper bags, irradiated by the sunlight for 3.25 hours. There were considerable number of sensitized spots on the films. But on 2 sheets of films irradiated for 30 minutes, no sensitized spot was found this time. c) Put films packed with black-paper bags in a room of normal condition for more than 72 hours. No sensitizing effect was found. The above experiments proved that there was no reliability problem for the black-ink-case packing. As for black-paper packing, if films packed in it are not irradiated by intense light for a long time, there will be no sensitizing effect on the films. The films used in experiments in black-paper packing are usually kept in a black bag, and taken out just before the experiments. For all of them, there is no chance to be exposed directly to sunlight. So, the possibility of film exposure due to improper packing methods can be eliminated.

(4) Discussion

(A) During the experiments, the Qigong masters themselves perceived 'Waiqi' penetrating the packing materials (the black paper or black-ink case) which enveloped the film. Factors such as the Qigong masters' mental state and environment have certain effects on the detecting probability.

(B) Results of the experimental groups showed that the Qigong 'Waiqi' can penetrate some medium and make the films sensitized. The sensitized spots are similar to diffracted spots of X-ray in crystals.

(C) Statistical results of the experiments show that the possibilities for film sensitizing effect by Qigong 'Waiqi' are less than 3.2% for black-ink-case packing, and less than 15.7% for black-paper packing.

(D) The results of experiments for the control groups eliminated the other factors which might cause film sensitization. Therefore, the sensitized spots on the films in our experiments were surely caused by Qigong 'Waiqi'.

Appendant Table 4.

Date	Name of Qigong Masters	Packing Materials	'Waiqi'-releasing Method	Number of Film	Result
Sept. 23, 1984	Ke Heng, Lin Yongle and 12 others	black-ink cases	with points Laogong and sword-fingers for 3 minutes	34	all not sensitized except one by Ke Heng with sword-finger releasing
Sept. 30, 1984	Lin Yongle Lin Yongle	black-paper bag	with Laogong point for 3 minutes	1	sensitized spots found
			with Tianchuan for 5 minutes; sword-fingers for 15 minutes	1 1	no sensitized spot found
Oct. 14	Lin Yongle	black-paper bag	with points: Laogong, Tianchuan five fingers (left), Yongquan (right), Zhu qiao, sword-fingers respectively for 10-45 minutes	10	sensitized spots found on 2 films and none on the others.
Oct. 1	Ke Heng	black-paper bag	with Laogong point for 5 minutes	3	none
Oct. 1	Ke Heng	black-ink case	with sword-fingers and Laogong point for 5 minutes	2	none
Oct. 1	Ke Heng	black-ink case	with Laogong point for 5 minutes	1	sensitized spots found
Oct. 1	Ke Heng	black-ink case	with Laogong point and sword fingers for 5 minutes	2	none
Oct. 1	Ke Heng	black-ink case	with laogong point for 5 minutes	1	none
Oct. 14	Ke Heng	black-ink case	with Laogong point for 5 minutes	3	sensitized spots found on 1 film
Oct. 14	Ke Heng	black-ink case	with Laogong point for 5 minutes	3	none

Note: Experiments were carried out in an underground hostel.

5. College Students' Experiences in Practising the Prenatal Energy Mobilizing Qigong

In September, 1987, with the support of the Administration of the Guangzhou College of Traditional Chinese Medicine, our Qigong Research Office organized and carried out Qigong teaching activities among the freshmen. Lectures on seven schools of Qigong were given to over 300 students in seven classes. The author was in charge of the teaching of the Prenatal Energy Mobilizing Qigong for 33 students in Class One of the Faculty of Traditional Chinese Medicine. Among them 5 were foreign students. After twenty-seven days of training and practising, the majority of students obtained obviously good effects of Qigong. The personal experiences of some students have been sorted out and devoted to our Qigong enthusiasts for their reference in practising the Prenatal Energy Mobilizing Qigong.

Chen Wei, male, aged 18: After practising the Prenatal Energy Mobilizing Qigong for seven days, I felt a bit thirsty and dizzy and had night emission for two nights running. The lecturer advised me to massage the points Yongquan (KI1) on both feet and emission did not occur in the following night.

Having practised Qigong for half a month, I had a relatively strong sensation of Qi in the Dai Meridian. The Dantian area became warm and heated. At that time, as soon as I had a slight mind-concentration, Qi sensation would appear in the points Laogong (PC8). Practising the pattern 'Interior Revolution of Qi in Dantian', I felt there was a round-shaped object of some weight in Dantian. At first the revolution of Qi was not so smooth. When mind-concentration was getting flagged, it revolved much more smoothly. Even if I forgot to count the number of circles, the circle was still turning round and round spontaneously. At that moment, it seemed to me that silence reigned everything and I had an extremely comfortable feeling. Since then, I have been feeling energetic. Even if I did not have a nap at noon, I was still as energetic and vigorous as usual so long as I practised the Quiescent Qigong for a while.

If, in the proceeding of practising Qigong, my mind was over-concentrated, the revolution of Qi would, on the contrary, became unsmooth. I felt as if my head was tightly hooped and swelling and almost immediately the revolution of Qi in Dantian stopped spontaneously. It remained still no matter how hard I tried to force it to revolve with my mind. Seeing this, I had to end my practice immediately. After I had practised Qigong for twenty-seven days, I felt the sensation of Qi in both of my hands and a very strong sensation of numbness all day. My temples kept beating and I felt Qi releasing from Baihui (DU20).

Shu Ping, male, aged 18: while I was practising the pattern 'Dantian-Mingmen Breathing', I had a hot sensation in the lower Dantian and Mingmen (DU 4). I felt a stream of Qi coming into my abdomen through the lower Dantian and the gastrointestinal peristalsis was quickened and I had a good appetite at meals. As the hot sensation in the lower abdomen became stronger, another hot sensation appeared in the waist and the back. Along with it, I felt very comfortable all over the body and had a pleasant state of mind. When I put the palms facing each other, I felt a very strong current of Qi forcing them apart. I immediately put my hands over my face to convey the Qi to my eyes to treat my myopia, short-sightness. Twenty-seven days later, the visual acuity of my left eye increased from 0.5 to 0.8 while the right one from 0.3 to 0.8. I changed my old spectacles, which was of 400 degrees, for a new ones of 200 degrees. I am resolved to try to get rid of my spectacles by practising Qigong for one more month.

Chen Yong Yuan, male, aged 18: Having practised Qigong for half a month, I felt my palms and Dantian become heated and I sweated all over during the practice, and saliva secretion increased. My appetite improved. My visual acuity of both eyes increased by 0.1 degree. But occasionally, such abnormal feelings as a confused train of thoughts made it difficult for me to tranquillize my mind and I felt swelling pains and dizziness in my head. But I managed to persist in my practice. After ten days, I could once again tranquillized my mind during Qigong practice and had a comfortable feeling and strong Qi sensation after being tranquillized. The abnormal reactions disappeared, too.

Liu Dong Yang, male, aged 17: Practising Qigong, I realized that the direction taken in the practice exerts a great influence on the effects of the practice. If you select a right direction, the Qi current will be especially smooth as if it was flowing freely along an unobstructed course and the extent of mind tranquillization will be the best, and it will be very easy for you to get into the state of Qigong.

Huang Xue Wu, male, aged 17: I closed my

eyes every time I practised the Quiescent Qigong Patterns. But it was obviously strange that each time I altered my direction without realizing it during my practice. After finishing the Ending Pattern, I opened my eyes to find that I was diverged from the original direction by an angle of 45 degree. After a half-month practice, there was obvious improvement in sleep and appetite, and my visual acuity was increased by 0.1 degree.

Yan Jin, male, aged 18: In the first few days of my practice, I found it difficult to concentrate my thoughts and there were too many distractions. I felt troublesome as to how and what to think in tranquillizing my mind. After over twenty days' training, I felt much better and persisted in my practice. "Failure is the mother of success" as a saying goes. My mind began to get tranquillized and my mental condition was getting improved and I began to feel the sensation of Qi and warmth in the lower Dantian.

He Wen Zhong, male, aged 18: When I was practising Qigong, I could not tranquillize my mind no matter how hard I tried, and distracting thoughts kept coming in. There was no response to the practice at all.

Li Xue Shan, male, aged 18: I was suffering from heart trouble. Every time I had strenuous exercises, a paroxysmal aching appeared in the precordial region. After practising Qigong, I had better mind-tranquillization. One month later, I felt no more paroxysmal cardiac aching.

Li Fei Teng, male, aged 20: I was very glad to see that my appetite and sleep were improved after a one-month Qigong practice. I became better self-controlled in handling my personal affairs. In the classroom, my attention could be easily concentrated and my visual acuity was increased by 0.4 degree.

Lin Han Ping, male, aged 21: I often suffered from gastrointestinal disorder and indigestion, and felt abdominal distention after meals and had frequent diarrhea. After practising Qigong for a month, I felt a Qi distending sensation in the lower Dantian and the points Laogong (P C 8) became heated and trembling from time to time, and had profuse secretion of saliva. I swallowed it, thinking that it was going straight down to the lower Dantian. The intestinal peristalsis was reinforced and digestion improved, and the bowel movements became normal. I felt more energetic than ever before.

Zhao Huan Jian, male, aged 22, a foreign

student: I was ill with chronic appendicitis and my right lower abdomen often ached. Having Practised Qigong for one month, the aching was greatly lessened and the appetite became better and sleep improved and I got a better memory. The visual acuity of my left eye was increased from 0.3 to 1.0 while the right one from 0.5 to 1.2. On September 28, I got a cold due to the attack of wind after sweating during Qigong practice. My tutor advised me to practise leg-crossed sitting in bed with an overcoat draped over my shoulders. Half an hour later, the whole body was heated and sweating, stiffness of the neck and headache disappeared promptly. So quickly came the effects as if clouds scattered by the wind and the bright sky came out again.

Yang Guang Ri, male, aged 22, a foreign student: After practising Qigong for twenty-seven days, I felt a stream of Heavenly Qi and Earthly Qi coming into my trunk and rather comfortable.

Tang Hai Feng, male, aged 25, a foreign student: I was very fond of playing basketball. During the games, if I ran too fast, I would have a very severe stuffy sensation in the chest. After practising Qigong for twenty days, the stuffy sensation disappeared and I felt that breathing was smoother than ever and I did not feel tired after playing ball game.

Huang Fei Ping, male, aged 17: When I practised Qigong, the secretion of saliva increased profusely. I felt that my body was so light as if it was floating in the air. I felt rather comfortable and my whole body became heated. The points Yongquan (KI1) at the soles of the feet were trembling and a sensation of ant-crawling travelling from Dantian to the palms. Before my eyes appeared white lights or a scene like paradise, and my body kept trembling all the time. To be true, I experienced sensations of all kinds. When I was practising the ending pattern, I felt that my Dantian had been replenished and I was full of vigor and vitality and got a good memory in particular.

Yuan Hui Lin, male, aged 48: I was a patient and fortunately attended the training course of Prenatal Energy Mobilizing Qigong with the approval from Mr. Xiao Xin He, lecturer of the Qigong Research Office in the Guangzhou College of Traditional Chinese Medicine. I had previously suffered from constipation for five years. Very often, I discharged goat-feces-like stool every other two or three days. Treatments with Chinese and western medicine showed no effect on my constipation. After attending the Qigong training course, I persisted in practising three times a day in the morning, at noon and in the evening. Each practice lasted thirty minutes. Half a month later, my bowel movement became normal, once daily and I was in very good spirit.

Pan Jin Hui, male, aged 19: I had a profound experience of the Prenatal Energy Mobilizing Qigong. In the first few days of my practice, I felt nothing but I was in good mood and full of vigor after practising. When I first practised the Quiescent Qigong Pattern Series with standing pose, my legs ached due to a long standing. But I felt more and more relaxed as days went by. At the beginning, I could not become tranquillized after reading silently the Instructions in verse for several times. Now only by reading it once I can enter the quiescent state of mind. When I first practised the pattern 'Deep Exhaling and Inhaling', I felt nothing in Dantian. Several days later, I got a very warm and comfortable feeling in Dantian and in the following days, the warmth became heat. In cold days, I placed my hands in front of Dantian and practised Qigong for a while, my hands would turn pleasantly warm and seemed swelling. Practising the pattern ' Nine Patterns for Inducing the Large

Circulation of Qi', I felt a stream of Qi moving inside the body with the movements. Most obviously when I practised the pattern ' JAI YAO YU DAI', Strengthening the Function of the Dai Meridian, my waist, very often, moved spontaneously, involving the movement of the body. After the practice, the whole body was pleasantly comfortable and I was soberminded. Attention became easily concentrated and I felt reading and reciting became easier than before, and I had quick wits. I had less distractions and fell asleep easily.

But on the other hand, I also experienced failure in the practice of the Quiescent Qigong Patterns. Sometimes I was overanxious for quick results and breathing was not so soft, long, slow, even and natural as it is required to be and occasionally I was in blind pursuit of deep breathing, which caused distention of Qi and affected the effectiveness of Qigong practice.

6. Experiences of the Clinical Application of the Prenatal Energy Mobilizing Qigong

By Yao Xian Wen

The Prenatal Energy Mobilizing Qigong, which originated from the Taoist School of Mount Ermei in Shichuan Province, was for Taoists to cultivate their morality and virtue according to the doctrine of Taoism. Three years ago, I was fortunate enough to learn this Qigong from Master **Ke Heng**. In the past few years, I practised this Qigong Pattern Series frequently and became a passionate lover of it. This Qigong Exercise is easy to learn, quick to acquire sensation of Qi-movement and to accumulate a great volume of Qi and it is rare to cause deviation in Qigong practice. This Qigong Exercise consists of a series of patterns which are closely linked to one another, starting from the simple to the complex, integrating the Motioned Patterns with the Quiescent Patterns to afford the greatest delight in the proceeding of practice.

The Quiescent Qigong Pattern Series can be classified into twelve methods for cultivating Qi, such as: inhaling, gathering, mobilizing, holding, stopping, accumulating, cultivating, transporting, regulating, releasing, collecting, and swallowing. The Motioned Qigong Patterns are divided into a series of nine with pleasant and flexible movements and great flow of Qi. The greatest advantage of this Qigong exercise is the word 'revolving'. It induces revolution of Inner Qi throughout the body. The Inner Qi can be conducted to revolve around the focus of diseases wherever they are. The practitioners will feel a relaxed sensation wherever the revolving-Qi goes, thus treating the diseases. Whereas, the sufficient Inner Qi can also be conveyed to the exterior and be released to treat other patients. Usually satisfactory therapeutic effectiveness is achieved in clinical application of Qigong. Herewith, I would like to give two examples to other Qigong practitioners for their reference.

Case 1: Patient Huang, male, aged 55, had a history of gastralgia for fifteen years and suffered from gastric hemorrhage twice. In the last two years, his health had been declining and the symptoms had worsened. He looked emaciated in body shape, sallow in complexion, with a continuous epigastralgia which became more severe in hunger, accompanied by the symptoms of anorexia, eructation, and oxyrygmia. Examinations by gastroscopy indicated gastroduodenal ulcer and chronic superficial gastritis. Both Chinese and western medicine were used but no signs of improvement were observed. In a hope, the patient made up his mind to learn and practise Qigong. The Prenatal Energy Mobilizing Qigong was taught. The patterns selected were: 'Deep Exhaling and Inhaling', 'Interior Revolution of Qi in Dantian' of the Quiescent Qigong Pattern Series, and the patterns of the Motioned Qigong: 'HUN DUN CU KAI', 'JIA YAO YU DAI' and 'JIU JIU GUI ZHEN'. After a half-month practice, he felt it easy to tranquillize his mind and the symptoms got alleviated. Having practised Qigong for a month, he could induce the circulation of Inner Qi. Each time after practising the patterns 'JIA YAO YU DAI' and 'JIU JIU GUI ZHEN', he purposely guided the Qi current to the epigastric cavity and revolved 36 turns clockwise and 36 turns counterclockwise. He felt the epigastric cavity extremely warm and comfortable. A two-month Qigong practice enabled him to relieve himself of all the symptoms he had previously suffered from and to have a gain in body weight. A follow-up examination showed the healing of gastric ulceration (in scaring stage). No relapse has ever been observed since he began to practise Qigong a year ago.

Case 2: Patient Chen, famale, aged 32, married, had a low fever lasting for two years and no obvious inducing factors were found upon examination two years ago. Often appeared such symptoms as a low fever in the afternoon, slight aversion to cold before the onset of fever, a feeling of tiredness and sleepiness, loss of weight and pale face. No organic and pathologic changes were discovered in accessory examination. Her illness was diagnosed by physicians in the Affiliated Hospital of Sun Yat-sen University of Medical Sciences as disorder of the automatic nervous function. But the treatments proved ineffective. So she turned to Qigong. But the patient always felt depressed sorrow and melancholy. In view of this, only the 'Foundation-laying' Pattern and 'Exhaling and Inhaling' Pattern were taught. After practising these patterns for more than a month, the patient's mental state was improved but the symptoms remained unchanged. Then the Motioned Qigong Pattern Series were added and the patient was advised to persevere with her practice. Two months later, the attack of fever only came every other three to five days.

During the course of practice, the patient felt a greater volume of Qi and both of her palms heated. There was a warm feeling in the lower abdomen. Her health condition was greatly improved after a three-month Qigong practice, all the symptoms disappeared and no relapse has been observed ever since.

7. Remarkable Improvement in My Cardiac Function by Practising the Prenatal Energy Mobilizing Qigong

By Lin Xi

I suffered from severe coronary heart disease. In 1983, the condition was even worse. I had an abrupt high fever with complication of cardiac infraction and went into shock soon after. I was immediately sent to the First Affiliated Hospital of Sun Yat-sen University of Medical Sciences for emergency treatment. After recovery, I was so weak that I could not take care of myself and felt general discomfort once I had a mild movement. Occasionally, I went out for a walk but I felt stuffiness in the chest and tired after walking a distance less than 500 meters and had to stop for a rest. Although I had been taking drugs prescribed by the doctor yet it seemed that the treatment was ineffective. I was rather worried and depressed. It was not long before I was introduced to the Qigong Master, *Ke Heng*, and he began to teach me some patterns of the Quiescent Qigong of the Prenatal Energy Mobilizing Qigong. I have persevered with my Qigong practice ever since. After a period of practice, I soon achieved good results. I had a good appetite and I could sleep well at night. Walking was more steady than before.

Moreover, my endurance strengthened. From then on, I had a much stronger belief in the Qigong's function of treating diseases and strengthening the body. I found myself bound to the Prenatal Energy Mobilizing Qigong. After practising Qigong at home for some time, I was able to walk to the Guangzhou Martyrs' Park to attend the Qigong Training Class run by the Qigong masters Chen Yan Feng and Ke Heng. I attended the Training Class twice and got an over-all training from the Quiescent Qigong Pattern Series to the Motioned Qigong Pattern Series. I felt my physical endurance had been prolonged and the resistance against diseases strengthened. The usual symptoms of common cold, arthritis, discomfort and stuffiness of the chest have been relieved. I can not only move about freely without any discomfort but also can walk for several hours.

These are the practical benefits brought to me by the Prenatal Energy Mobilizing Qigong in recuperating my health. I felt through my own practice that the Prenatal Energy Mobilizing Qigong is indeed worthy of popularizing and applying in terms of public health care.

8. The Cure of My Rhinitis by Practising the Prenatal Energy Mobilizing Qigong

By He Huo Xing

I am thirty-two years old but I have been ill with rhinitis for over twenty years. I used to have nasal obstruction, rhinorrhea and reversion of nasal discharge into the throat and aching in both ears, involving the occiput, swelling pain on both sides of the nose bridge accompanied with tinnitus, insomnia and listlessness. I have suffered a great deal from this prolonged illness. As a result, my work and study were both affected. Although I sought treatment through every possible means and kept taking medicine for a long time, yet the treatments proved ineffective and I suffered much mental agony. Later I went and asked for Qigong treatment from Master Ke Heng. Soon the symptoms were improved but my rhinitis had not yet been eliminated. Master *Ke Heng* encouraged me to learn the Prenatal Energy Mobilizing Qigong.

At the end of 1985, I acknowledged *Ke Heng* as my Qigong tutor and learned these Qigong patterns earnestly. After practising Qigong for over a year, there was a great improvement in my condition and the symptoms such as headache, tinnitus, insomnia and swelling pain of the nose bridge all disappeared. What is more, nasal discharge was reduced greatly.

In addition, my gastritis also disappeared and my lip-ulceration was obviously relieved after a three-month Qigong practice. Early in 1987, my weight increased 5 kgs more than before and I was full of vigor. It was through my own experience that I realized that the practice of these Qigong patterns exerts a comprehensive regulating effect on my bodily function and it is the Prenatal Energy Mobilizing Qigong that enables me to regain happiness and joy.

9. A Letter of Thanks by a Japanese Student Studying in China

Dear editors of the Yang Cheng Wanbao:

I used to suffer from severe myopia. Upon a five-meter visual acuity test, the visual acuity of my both eyes was confirmed to be 0.06. After the treatment of Qigong by the Qigong Master **Ke Heng** in the Youth Beauty and Health-Care Department, Guangzhou Research Institute of Stomatologic and Plastic Surgery for fifty days, the visual acuity of both eyes was reconfirmed 0.7. There was an incredible increase. Before the treatment, I had to wear my spectacles when I went cycling. After the treatment, I did not have to wear my spectacles any more.

Herewith, I would like to express my heartfelt gratitude through you to Mr. Ke Heng and all the staffs in the Youth Beauty and Health-Care Clinic.

Sincerely yours
Men Xie Sheng
A Japanese student of Jinan University

10. Answers to the Questions from Readers

Q: Why is it called the 'Prenatal Energy Mobilizing Qigong'?

A: Essence of life, Qi (vital enegy), vitality, these three essential substances constituting the human body and maintaining life activities are called respectively YUAN JING (prenatal essence), YUAN QI (primordial energy), YUAN SHEN (primary vitality) in terms of the theory of traditional Chinese medicine. Yuan in Chinese denotes the meaning ' primitive or prenatal' acquired before birth, while the essence is stored in the five Zang organs (heart, liver, spleen, lung and kidney). In its primitive state, without shape, it is called YUAN JING (prenatal essence). If it takes shape, it is the acquired essence (the essential substances derived from food and used to maintain the vital activities and metabolism of the body). YUAN QI (primordial energy), acting as the primary motive force for life activities, circulates through the meridian system to all parts of the body. YUAN SHEN (primary vitality) refers to the functions of the human body and the cerebrum. In motion, it refers to the mentality, consciousness and thinking, etc.. In the ' Scripture on Elixir of Life', the code for essence is water; for vitality is fire; while Qi can be classified into two types: the Prenatal Qi and Postnatal Qi. The Prenatal Energy Mobilizing Qigong is to transform the postnatal Qi into prenatal Qi by means of cultivating and tempering so as to make JING QI (refined energy) condensed and vapoured to circulate along the routes of the Ren and Du Meridians. As is expected, cultivated and tempered for a long period of time, the Essence, Qi and Vitality would be condensed into an elixir, which has the functions of preventing and treating diseases, strengthening the body and prolonging life.

Q: If I start practising the Prenatal Energy Mobilizing Qigong, how often do I have to practise every day and how long should I practise each time?

A: The time and duration vary from person to person. Those who have chronic diseases and those who are retired can practise more often. Those who have jobs and busy schedules can practise less. Generally speaking, you can practise the Motioned Qigong Pattern Series; Nine Patterns for Inducing the Large Circulation of Qi for about thirty minutes in the morning and the Quiescent Qigong Pattern Series at noon or in the evening for twenty to forty minutes. It would be adequate for those who are healthy and have busy schedules to practise the Motioned Qigong Patterns in the morning and the Quiescent Qigong Patterns at night for ten to twenty minutes each time.

Q: There are many patterns in Quiescent Qigong of

the Prenatal Energy Mobilizing Qigong. Is it good to practise all of them or just select one or two of them? Which pattern should be selected for our practice?

A: When Master *Chen Yan Feng* taught Mr. *Ke Heng* this Qigong, he advised *Ke Heng* to practise ' Dantian-Mingmen Breathing' (deep exhaling-inhaling method) for one year first. It was not until he got a heated sensation in Dantian could he be taught to practise the pattern ' Interior Revolution of Qi in Dantian'. The rest of the patterns in the Quiescent Qigong Pattern Series were developed and systemized by Mr. *Ke Heng* later in his own practice. These two patterns are the foundation of the Quiescent Qigong. Whereas, the pattern ' Interior Revolution of Qi in Dantian' is the principal one in the Quiescent Qigong. Beginners can start with these two patterns. But it needs not take two years. Every night before going to bed, you can first practise the pattern ' Dan-Ming Breathing' for ten minutes. When you are mentally tranquillized, practise the pattern ' Interior Revolution of Qi in Dantian' four to eight rounds (about twenty minutes) till the exhaling becomes sounldess and fine and the inhaling soft, slow and lengthy. By doing so every night, you will become much more skillful in the practice and you can master Qigong so well as days go by that the Prenatal Qi will be accumulated and condensed gradually and finally be transformed into 'elixir' of life. If you have enough time you may as well start from the beginning and practise the whole series of the Quiescent Qigong Patterns.

Q: Every time I practised the pattern 'Interior Revolution of Qi in Dantian', there was an itching sensation in the Dantian area. Do you think it is a favourable omen or a bad one?

A: Practising the Prenatal Energy Mobilizing Qigong, as in other Qigong exercises, practitioners will usually experience the following sensations: such as numbness, swelling, hotness, itching, ant-crawling, emptiness, relaxation, floating, sourness and an increase in saliva secretion, wind-blowing and slight trembling. These sensations are what we call 'Eight-Touches', but in fact, more than eight. They are normal reactions in the practice of Qigong. The reactions to Qigong are different from person to person. When you practised the pattern 'Interior Revolution of Qi in Dantian', the itching sensation in Dantian was in fact the manifestation of 'gaining-Qi', a normal phenomenon. What you have to do is to free your mind from doubts and misgivings and not to follow it but just let it develop naturally.

Q: What does it mean by saying 'Wherever the mind is concentrated, follow will the Qi, the sole pursuit is the extreme nothingness state of mind'?

A: What we are talking about here is the interrelationship betwen the mind and Qi and also that between mind-Qi and nothingness, a high extent of mind-tranquillization. The phrase 'wherever the mind is concentrated' refers to the leading role played by the mind, which serves as the purpose for concentrating the mind. Acted upon by the effect exerted by the concentrated-mind, Qi circulates along with the mind, being in a subordinate status. But to a certain extent will Qi surpass the mind. 'The sole pursuit is the extreme nothingness state of mind' means that after the Qi is mobilized and stimulated, it gets more active, sometimes the Qi circulates faster than the mind. In this case, spontaneous moving of the body will usually occur. We call this phenomenon as 'Qi will surpass the mind to a certain extent' because at this stage, Qi is playing a leading role.

Therefore, the mind will in turn follow the Qi in its circulation. 'The sole purpose is the ultimate nothingness state of mind' means under any circumstances should a practitioner bear in mind that his sole pursuit is the nothingness state of mind. No matter which one plays the leading role, the mind or the Qi, he should neither fear it nor pay any attention to it, but remain unruffled and act as if nothing has ever happened. But above all, only in the Qigong state of nothingness can be ensured the mutual dependence between Qi and mind, and may the primordial vitality take shape and appear. From this we can see what an important place nothingness takes in the interrelationship between the mind and Qi.

Q: I am sixty years old, of delicate constitution and ill with several diseases. What posture should I take when practising the pattern 'Interior Revolution of Qi in Dantion'?

A: Practising this pattern, you might as well take anyone, standing, sitting or lying. Generally, the sitting pose is the best and the leg-crossed sitting pose in particular, which gives much stronger sensation of Qi. Those who are young and healthy can take the standing posture. It is advisable for the old and the sick and those with delicate constitution to take the lying posture. Whatever posture you take, it should meet the requirements of making yourself comfortable and natural.

Q: While I was practising the pattern 'Interior Revolution of Qi in Dantian', I could not tranquillize my mind occassionally. Will it be all right just to let my thought circle along with the revolving Qi in Dantian?

A: If your mind could circle along with the revolution of Qi within the the light ring in Dantian, that means your mind has already been tranquillized. Even if there are still some distractions, the revolving light ring can also induce you to enter a tranquillized state of mind. This is what we mean 'mind accompanying with Qi'. It does not matter if your mind can not be tranquillized for the moment so long as your attention can be concentrated, the focus of attention will surely result in tranquillization of mind.

Q: What should be the next step after succeeding in the practice of 'Interior Revolution of Qi in Dantian'?

A: The practice of 'Interior Revolution of Qi in Dantian' is to build up a linkage between the mind and Qi. It is a good way to temper the Qi and to condense it into the elixir of life.

When the revolution of Qi produces a sensation of warmth, fullness and swelling in Dantian, it will give rise to the phenomenon of overflow of Qi due to excess, the leaking of Qi. The phenomenon fully manifests that the 'Interior Revolution of Qi in Dantian' is tending to a much higher stage of the practice. By this time, the Qi in Dantian has already been reinforced and is strong enough that one can proceed to the practice of 'Longitudinal Revolution of Qi from Dantian'. For those who are sensitive to Qigong, after the success in the practice of 'Interior Revolution of Qi in Dantian', the phenomenon of 'Longitudinal Revolution of Qi from Dantian' will spontaneously appear: the Primordial Qi starts circulating from the Du Meridian to the Ren Meridian, forming an endless circulation of Qi, which is called 'the Small Circulation of Qi'.

Q: Can emission be treated by practising the Prenatal Energy Mobilizing Qigong? During the practice, is it favourable to take Chinese medicine as a supplementary treatment? Is it abnormal that emission happens during the period of Qigong practice? When will be the ideal time for Qigong practice?

A: The practice of this Qigong is applicable to emission because practising the Motioned Qigong Pattern Series can strengthen the constitution and maintain the balance of Yin and Yang. The practice of 'Interior Revolution of Qi in Dantian' has the function of strengthening the kidney to benefit the marrow. It is much more effective for emission due to deficiency of Kidney-Yang. For those ill with emission caused by masturbation, only by making a resolve to give up the bad habit of masturbation can Qigong practice take effect. For those suffering from severe emission, it is not contradictory but necessary to combine medical treatments with Qigong practice during the period of practice. The application of Qigong and Chinese medicine both aim at enabling the patients to maintain the equilibrium of Yin and Yang so that the cure of diseases can be expected. Do not worry about reoccurrence of emission during the period of Qigong practice. This is, in most cases, caused by the excess of sperms. This is regarded as spermatorrhea due to overflow of the seminal vesicle, which is a normal physiological phenomenon. The medical classics 'Secrets of Chamber's Affairs' says that' a man of twenty has spermatorrhea once every four days; a man of thirty once every eight days; men at the age of forty once every sixteen days; those of fifty once every twenty days'. These are the normal physiological phenomena and also the limit for sexual life. Those who are intending to lay a solid foundation of Qigong within one hundred days are strictly prohibited to have sexual intercourse. Even if those with quite a sound foundation of Qigong should also have a moderate sexual life. If abnormal emission occurs during the period of Qigong practice, the cause should be tracked down and adequate treatments should be given. In case of emission caused by deficiency of Yin and hyperactivity of fire, practitioners are advised to massage the points Yongquan (KI1) on both feet thirty-six times till they are heated. Generally, the ideal time for the treatment of emission by practising 'Interior Revolution of Qi in Dantian' is the You Period (5:00p.m. to 7:00p.m.) because the circulation of Qi and blood of the Kidney Meridian is the most vigorous. If it is inconvenient, the Shen Period (3:00p.m. to

5:00p. m.) can be selected instead for the Qi and blood circulate the most vigorously through the Urinary Bladder Meridian at this period and the Kidney Meridian has an exterior— interior relationship with the Urinary Bladder Meridian.

Q: I am suffering from several diseases such as tuberculosis, gastric ulcer, chronic hepatitis, indigestion and neurasthenia and in poor health. Can the practice of Prenatal Energy Mobilizing Qigong be a miraculous cure of them?

A: Most Qigong exercises are effective for a variety of chronic diseases. Qigong Master Ke Heng himself once suffered from six different diseases. But he persevered in practising Qigong. All were cured in only two years. According to our experiences in teaching Qigong in recent years, we have concluded that this Qigong has therapeutic effectiveness to some extent for the following diseases (see Table 5).

Appendant Table 5

Classification	Diseases and Symptoms
Cardiovascular system	rheumatic heart disease, hypertension, hypotension, cerebral arteriosclerosis, paralysis
Respiratory system	pulmonary tuberculosis, pulmonary emphysema, bronchitis, bronchus asthma, pneumosilicosis, sternocostal pains
Digestive system	gastric ulcer, duodenal ulcer, chronic gastritis, gastroptosis, indigestion, early hepatocirrhosis, chronic cholecystitis
Urinary and reproductive system	chronic nephritis, diabetes, impotence, emission, prospermia, lumbago due to deficiency of kidney
Osteoarthropathy	vertebral degenerative hypertrophy, arthritis, periarthritis of shoulder
Gynopathy	irregular menses, leukorrhea, chronic pelvic cellulitis
Others	chronic laryngitis, chilblain, myopia, tumor, adiposis, facial ecchymoses

Q: Should the waistband be tightened or loosened when practising the Prenatal Energy Mobilizing Qigong?

A: No matter what Qigong patterns you are practising, the Motioned Qigong Patterns or the Quiescent Qigong Patterns, it is better to loosen the waistband or belt and the other things tightened on the body, such as wrist watch, brassiere and ring, etc. should be removed or loosened so as not to affect the free flow of the Interior Qi.

Q: After I practised the Prenatal Energy Mobilizing Qigong for ten days, I had a dryness in the mouth, sore throat, dizziness and restlessness. Are these phenomena of deviations? Can I continue my practice?

A: First of all, you should rectify your recognition of deviation. Many books on Qigong state that deviations should be prevented and people are very worried about the occurrence of deviations during the proceeding of Qigong practice. When Qigong Master Yan Xin addressed the audience of over a hundred thousand in his two lectures given in Guangzhou in December, 1987 and January, 1988 respectively, he said, "There is not such a word, 'deviation' in Qigong. What people call deviations can only be referred to special reactions to Qigong. They are, in fact, the preludes of attacks of Qi on the focus, the heightening of the effect of Qi or the functioning of Qi, or in other words, they are reactions caused by the diseased Qi from your family members or people around you when the

Qi is eliminated through your body. " Therefore, you can set your mind at ease when practising Qigong. Do not worry excessively as long as you are mentally tranquillized and bodily completely relaxed. Apart from these, based on our analysis of the patterns of the Prenatal Energy Mobilizing Qigong, sixty percent of them have the function of invigorating Yang; forty percent have the function of nourishing Yin. It is concluded that this Qigong Pattern Series is inclined to invigoration of Yang. Only three percent of practitioners who belong to the sensitive type or those with symptoms of hyperactivity of Yang Qi will have the above syndromes. These are not deviations of Qigong but manifestations of hyperactivity of fire.

So long as practitioners concentrate their minds on points Yongquan (KI1) or apply massage to Yongquan point of the right foot with the left palm or to the left with the right palm till they are heated, the symptoms of hyperactivity of fire will disappear spontaneously. I would like to illustrate this point with the following examples:

CASE 1. *Yan Ai Qun*, female, aged 19, a student of Grade 86.

She said: When I first practised the Prenatal

Energy Mobilizing Qigong, I felt my throat aching and got feverish sensation in the Five Centres: the palms, soles and the chest, and I lost my temper easily. After practising the Ending Pattern, I massaged the Yongquan points with my palms, the symptoms were immediately relieved. I realized that this Qigong is inclined to the invigoration of Yang.

CASE 2. *Jiang Ming*, male, aged 19, a student of Grade 86.

When talking about experiences in practising Qigong, he said, 'Each time after Qigong practice, I felt a warm current of Qi flowing at the waist and the back, and the whole body became hot. When I practised the Quiescent Qigong Patterns with standing posture, my body would quiver. When practised with leg-crossed sitting pose, the limbs would first become heated, swelling and numb. Soon afterwards, I could not feel where my limbs were as if they had disappeared. Sometimes after practice, I felt a dryness in the mouth, a sore throat and headache. When these symptoms occurred, I concentrated my mind on points Yongquan. A day later, these feelings were all gone. I learnt from my own experiences that mind-concentration on or massaging the points

Yongquan has the functions of 'providing water for suppressing fire' and inducing fire to return to its origin according to the theory of Five Elements of traditional Chinese medicine.

CASE 3. *Deng Wei*, male, aged 18, a student of Grade 87.

He wrote in his paper, "I had practised 'Pillar-standing Pose' of Chinese boxing for several years and got a primary foundation. Therefore, when I began to practise the Prenatal Energy Mobilizing Qigong, I felt a flow of Qi descending from Dantian to the perineum and then ascending through the point Changqiang (DU1). When practising the Quiescent Qigong Patterns, I felt a sensation of heat in Dantian as soon as I began, but there were many distractions in my mind, which was hard to tranquillize. In the early stage, I was a bit overanxious for quick results. When my classmates applied remote control over me, I imagined absorbing their 'Waiqi' and also imagined the Qi coming out of their Baihui points (DU20) and entering my body. This resulted in sthenia of Yang-Fire, causing dryness in the mouth and of the tongue and a very strong sensation of Qi on the hands. As soon as my hands got near to an object, I felt hot in the points Laogong (PC8). I stopped my practice for several days and went to consult the tutor. He instructed me to practise palm-to-palm with a girl student. I once again used my concentrated mind to induce her Qi into my body through Laogong points (P C 8). As was expected, a flow of cool Qi raided into my Laogong points and travelled directly into my trunk. After practice, I felt rather comfortable. But the next day, I fell ill suddenly. I soon found out that the girl classmate was ill at that time and her diseased Qi was transferred to my body through the practice. Later I adopted the method of absorbing the Earthly Yin Qi. When I practised the pattern WU QI CHAO YUAN and the pattern HUN DUN CU KAI, while making the hand-ascending gesture, I used my imagination to conduct Qi to ascend from points Yongquan (KI1) into Dantian. This method was really so miraculous that the above mentioned symptoms all disappeared. Yin and Yang were rebalanced and I was getting stronger and stronger."

中国先天一元气功

陈炎烽　柯　衡　肖鑫和　著
刘启和　康寿芷　陈学诗　译
责任编辑　陈　岩

*

中国广东科技出版社出版
中国广东科技出版社电脑室排版
（中国广州环市东路水荫路11号13楼）
中国广东新华印刷厂印刷
（中国广州永福路45号）
中国国际图书贸易总公司发行
（中国北京车公庄西路21号）
北京邮政信箱第399号　邮政编码100044
1992年（大32开）第1版（英文版）　1992年第1次印刷
ISBN7- 5359- 0756- 3/R・144（外）
00560
14- E- 2589P